1991

Teaching Writing

Teaching Writing

Pedagogy, Gender, and Equity

edited by

Cynthia L. Caywood
and
Gillian R. Overing

STATE UNIVERSITY OF NEW YORK PRESS

Published by
State University of New York Press, Albany

© 1987 State University of New York

For information, address State University of New York
Press, State University Plaza, Albany, N.Y., 12246

Library of Congress Cataloging in Publication Data

Teaching writing.

   Bibliography: p.
   Includes index.
   1. English language—Rhetoric—Study and teaching.
2. English language—Sex differences. 3. Sex
discrimination in education. 4. Sexism in language.
5. Feminism. 6. Women—Education. 7. Women—Language.
8. Interdisciplinary approach in education.
I. Caywood, Cynthia L., 1952-   . II. Overing,
Gillian R., 1952-   .
PE1404.T4   1987   808'.042'07   86-14520
ISBN 0-88706-352-7
ISBN 0-88706-353-5 (pbk.)

10 9 8 7 6 5 4 3 2

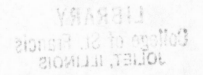

Contents

Contents

Chapter V: Equity Across the Curriculum:
The Administrator's Challenge

Acknowledgments

We would like to thank Wake Forest University, the Duke-UNC Women's Resource Center, and the University of San Diego for providing us with the funding and secretarial help which made this project possible. Specifically, we would like to thank Nancy Durham and Mildred Garris, formerly secretaries in the Wake Forest University English Department and Monica Wagner and Philomena Stein, manuscript secretaries at the University of San Diego. We would also like to thank our student assistants, Leslie Mizell, Phil Woods, and Cherrie Lamb for their tireless and conscientious attention to mundane detail; our colleagues in the Wake Forest University Women's Studies Program, especially Nancy Cotton, Dolly McPherson, and Peggy Smith, for their committed support and valuable comments; and our contributors, whose enthusiasm for this project has matched our own.

Introduction

Cynthia L. Caywood and Gillian R. Overing

We are both teachers of writing, concerned with equity in our classrooms. Equity does not mean to us the abolition of differences among individuals, nor does it imply a blanket imposition of an Orwellian homogeneity. It does not mean stifling some voices so that others may be heard; it does not demand the compromising of academic standards in the name of egalitarianism. Equity, as we understand it, creates new standards which accommodate and nurture differences. Equity fosters the individual voice in the classroom, investing students with confidence in their own authority. Equity unleashes the creative potential of heterogeneity. This definition of equity is at the heart of this anthology, and our attempts as teachers to model our pedagogy on this principle provided the impetus for assembling it.

Although this project officially began with a nationwide call for papers distributed to over 300 colleges, it originated in casual, informal conversations about how we teach and what we believe. As we moved towards reconciling these, certain formal academic questions began to arise. At what point did our parallel interests in feminism and revisionist writing theory converge? How could we realize in both theory and practice our intuitive understanding of their fundamental connection? We began to search for scholarship on the relationship between feminist theory and the teaching of writing, and we discovered that it was a relatively unexplored area. Existing scholarship was largely devoted to language study and textbook selection.

While these were important issues, they did not address directly what we thought were the most important ones: basic pedagogical theory and philosophical approaches to the teaching of writing as these involve questions of equity. The teacher's approach itself, we felt, had to be central to the issue of equity.

The anthology is an exploration of the relationship between feminist theory and writing theory. In assembling it and reviewing these two bodies of research, we have discovered a consistent pattern, one characterized by the recurrent intersection of several major premises at the heart of both bodies of research. The most important of these are: the relation between revisionist critiques of traditional writing theory and the feminist critique of masculinist, patriarchal ways of being; and the correlation between the revisionists' restructuring of pedagogy and revaluing of the student and feminists' restructuring of cultural models and revaluing of the experience of women.

The familiar revisionist view of writing as process, which challenges the classical view of writing as product, offers a paradigmatic dialectic also appropriate to feminist discourse. The model of writing as product is inherently authoritarian. The act of writing becomes a suppressed and private activity of the self which is eventually divorced from the product made public. As a result, certain forms of discourse and language are privileged: the expository essay is valued over the exploratory; the argumentative essay set above the autobiographical; the clear evocation of a thesis preferred to a more organic exploration of a topic; the impersonal, rational voice ranked more highly than the intimate, subjective one. The valuing of one form over another requires that the teacher be a judge, imposing a hierarchy of learned aesthetic values, gathered from ideal texts, upon the student text.

Feminist theory in general questions the inherently authoritarian nature of patriarchy. In particular, the traditional notions of canonicity, "the eternal verity of the received standards of greatness or even goodness" (Robinson, 118), are challenged because they originate in masculinist aesthetic values. Feminist critics question the exclusion of alternate forms of discourse such as private poetry, letters, diaries, journals, personal narratives, oral or written, and autobiographies. These forms have been ignored because they are frequently the only forms of discourse available to women, and "women's literature and the female tradition tend to be evoked as an autonomous cultural experience, not impinging on the rest of literary history" (Robinson, 116). These private acts of writing and their exclusion from the public domain, or in this case, publication, are parallel to the suppression of the composing self necessitated by the product model. Feminist critics have also pushed this exploration of women's silence into the area of linguistic space, claiming that not only discourse forms but language itself are exclusive.

The model of writing as a process is less rigidly structured. Much more emphasis is given to the act of writing, to both revealing and examining the private process of discovery. One important result of this change of emphasis should be the validation of the private voice in that the process of discovery becomes as important, if not more so, than the summarized product of discovery. Revisionist writing theorists also affirm the importance of the inner voice, its forms of discourse, and its language: pre-writing, free writing, rough drafts and their revisions, learning logs, reading diaries, journals, and exploratory essays are as valued as the more traditional, linear modes of expression. The teacher, while she must eventually move into the role of evaluator, is more of a collaborator with the student in his struggle for "fluency," a term which includes generating ideas and information, selecting, focusing, getting started, composing, communicating, and correcting. When the teacher moves into the role of evaluator, her "ideal texts" are formed by both the experiences of the students and her authority as a more practiced and knowledgeable member of the learning community.

Just as process subsumes the principles of product into a larger definition of what writing is, the feminist restructuring of cultural models urges the same subsuming of exclusive masculinist aesthetics into larger conceptual frameworks that can include the full range of all human experience. Feminist critics who challenge the canon seek to redefine and make more inclusive the criteria for valuing and selection. Lillian Robinson argues that "the feminist challenge . . . has not been simply a reiterated attack, but a series of suggested alternatives to the male-dominated membership and attitudes of the accepted canon" (106). She continues by saying that the point of questioning and restructuring the canon, "is not to label and dismiss even the most sexist literary classics, but to enable all us to apprehend them, finally, in all their human dimensions" (118). Revising aesthetic criteria means taking seriously alternate discourse forms used by women which are in many cases identical to those forms revisionist writing theorists advocate as a means of validating the student's private voice. In short, both revisionist writing theorists and feminist critics recognize the equal value of private and public, of personalized experience and detached abstraction.

Revised notions of canonicity and re-valued forms of discourse demand an examination of language itself, and feminist critiques of language offer an especially charged debate. Some critics, especially the French, regard language as inseparable from patriarchical oppression. Such critics are convinced "that there can be no revolution without the disruption of the symbolic order—bourgeois language, the language of the old humanisms with their belief in a coherent subject—and that only by dislocating syntax, playing with the signifier, punning outrageously and constantly can the old language and the old order be subverted" (Marks and de Courtivron, 32-33). Others believe rather that "the problem is not that language is insufficient to express women's consciousness but that women have been denied the full resources of language and have been forced into silence, euphemism, or circumlocution" (Showalter, "Wilderness," 255). Between these extremes lie the attempts of other feminists to call attention to sexist biases in syntax and vocabulary and the inequalities of male-female verbal interactions. However feminists resolve the "problem" of language, its importance is as vital to them as to writing theorists.

We have discussed only a few of the connections between these two bodies of theory, but the point, we hope, is clear: the process model, insofar as it facilitates and legitimizes the fullest expression of the individual voice, is compatible with the feminist re-visioning of hierarchy, if not essential to it. In its exploration of this connection between the process model and feminist reconstruction of cultural models, the anthology, which includes essays that range from focused descriptions of classroom technique to more theoretical speculation, fleshes out the connections we have outlined above and develops many more. For example, recognizing the integrity of the personal voice in the public domain is reflected in Annas' blend of anecdote and abstraction; in Goulston's autobiographical account of her struggles as a woman scholar and her endorsing through word and action the validity of incorporating personal response into traditional expository modes; and in DeShazer's providing of models which allow students to do the same. The recognition of the value of alternate discourse forms is reflected in Quinn's use of digression in class discussion as a catalyst for the student's voice and in Perry's use of journals. The issue of language, both verbal and written, is taken up most specifically by Freed, Lavine, and Cowell. Restrictive pedagogical models are set against facilitative alternatives such as Däumer and Runzo's metaphor of teacher as mother, Stanger's advocacy and exploration of the collaborative dynamic, and Frey's non-confrontational, "peaceful," student-centered writing class.

Our anthology begins to provide some alternatives to inhibiting pedagogical models, and outlines the promising, initial stages of a new, coherent feminist discourse on writing. Although we realize that it may not meet some of the particular needs of minority students, we believe that it can be a useful pedagogical tool and meet a variety of demands, wherever and however writing is taught. Because we conceived of it as a source of information, we have organized the articles in such a way to facilitate easy reference, and have divided them into five generalized areas of emphasis. We have also included a bibliography.

Our goal in putting the anthology together has been to provide other writing teachers with a starting point in their reconsideration of their pedagogical methods. The writing course has the potential to be the single, most important learning experience for students if it provides them with confidence in their own ideas and belief in their own authority. We think our book can help teachers realize this potential, but writing teachers should not be alone in their concern for cultivating writing as a mode of learning. Therefore, we hope that the anthology will speak to a larger audience, to all who believe in the importance of writing in their classroom, and to those who acknowledge the essential role of writing in the individual's quest for self-definition.

Works Cited

Marks, Elaine and Isabelle de Courtivron, Eds. *New French Feminisms: An Anthology.* Amherst, MA: The University of Massachusetts Press, 1980.

Robinson, Lillian. "Treason our Text: Feminist Challenge to the Literary Canon." *The New Feminist Criticism: Essays on Women, Literature, and Theory.* Ed. Elaine Showalter. New York: Pantheon Books, 1985. 105-121.

Showalter, Elaine. "Feminist Criticism in the Wilderness." *The New Feminist Criticism: Essays on Women, Literature, and Theory.* Ed. Elaine Showalter. New York: Pantheon Books, 1985. 243-270.

Chapter I

Old Silences, New Voices

This chapter lays out some theoretical groundwork. The writers shape the larger critical context for the particular practical applications taken up in later chapters. The essays offer a survey of current research in the fields of feminism and writing theory and show various ways in which these two major bodies of research reinforce and inform each other. Their interrelation is examined in a variety of contexts: the problematic coalition of feminist theory and the personal difficulties of writing as a woman scholar; the integral and fundamental relation of equity in the classroom and collaborative learning; and mothering as a pedagogical model.

Silences: Feminist Language Research and the Teaching of Writing

Pamela J. Annas

> In you bottled up is a woman peppery as curry,
> a yam of a woman of butter and brass,
> compounded of acid and sweet like a pineapple,
> like a handgrenade set to explode,
> like goldenrod ready to bloom (Piercy, 247).[1]

In 1963, Betty Friedan remarked in *The Feminine Mystique* on "the problem that had no name." Two years later, Tillie Olsen named the problem that had no name as a problem *because* it had no name when her essay "Silences" appeared in *Harper's Magazine*. By the late 1960s, women were meeting in living rooms, kitchens, and unused classrooms all over the country in a form that soon came to be called the consciousness raising group. In those groups, women began to bridge isolation and break silence, narrating personal experiences, listening to the experiences of other women in the group, comparing and contrasting, finding the common threads, describing, analyzing, defining and giving names to recurring motifs in their lives. Not only did various social issues (equal pay for equal work, a woman's right to control over her own body, and so on) take shape in those discussions and become the content of a powerful social movement, but also a form of discourse emerged based on cooperation and augmentation rather than competitiveness, on dialogue rather than hierarchy. The beginnings of contemporary feminism are rooted in a recognition of the connections between expression and epistemology, naming and knowing, seeing and saying, forms of consciousness and the content of women's experience.

My students in "Writing as Women," an intermediate level writing course at the University of Massachusetts/Boston, talk a lot about silence: about what kinds of silence there are: the voices inside you that tell you to be quiet, the voices outside you that drown you out or politely dismiss what you say or do not understand you, the silence inside you that avoids saying anything important even to yourself, internal and external forms of censorship, and the stress that it produces. One student in the class (Karen) wrote:

Silence and tension. Words and fury. These are connected for me. When there is a lull in the class discussion in Writing as Women or when silence is discussed, I feel like I'm going to explode. . . . I battle with myself whether or not to speak. "I should plan out what I'm going to say," I'll sometimes think to myself. After all, I don't want to take up class time making stupid comments. Sometimes I'll even make a contract with myself before class that I'll have to speak in class that night. Usually I'll wait until almost the end of class when my tension is built up. I'll open my mouth and like a firecracker set off my words will come [out] garbled and loud. My voice will sound rusty.[2]

In a class discussion of writing blocks, one student said, "I realize that what I'm writing is coming from a deep place, and it's making me look at me in a way I've never looked at me before, and it's frightening because I don't know what I'm going to see there; so I stop."[3] When we did a free association on the word "silence," one of the responses was "staying out of trouble." Writing (or speaking) is taking a risk, and the more specifically and concretely one writes the bigger the risk. A student wrote: "When I write publicly [as opposed to writing in her journal], I put on [a] thick plastic mask. I wedge a wall between myself and what I write. It's better to write abstractly about something I don't care about. Then I don't have to show how I feel. And others won't be able to tell a thing about me." Another student hoped that the class would be a way for her to move "out of the hidden private world of journal entries." A woman who is in the class this semester (Julie) remembered that one of the first poems she ever wrote, when she was eleven years old, was called "Silence." Though she takes herself very seriously now as a poet, writing in a disciplined way and sending her work out to poetry magazines, she remarked in a paper:

> I used to say I wrote poetry because it was the only thing I could do well, as if I were ashamed of writing, as if it were less of an achievement to have written a poem than to have a date every Saturday night. I still have trouble seeing myself as a woman who writes. I am not certain I know what that means. I have subverted, delayed, camouflaged, disowned, betrayed, concealed, and hidden my own writing.

And a woman in her forties (Selena), who worked all day and came to this writing class at night, wrote: "As a wife and a working mother, my day is filled with such things as washing clothes, ironing, cleaning, cooking, and trying to help my children with their homework or aid them in solving a problem that they may have encountered during the day. My husband also requires some of my time. He once said, 'I married a woman not a book'. . . .A combination of all these things affects me and the writing that I never do. I just don't have the time." As Tillie Olsen remarks in *Silences*, "motherhood means being instantly interruptable, responsive, responsible. . . .Work interrupted, deferred, relinquished, makes blockage" (18-19).

I have structured into the course writing exercises and class discussions that attempt to connect students with the complexity of who they are, that make writing a less mysterious and more familiar enterprise, and that move them from silence to words and from private to public writing. The first exercise asks them to describe either a positive or a negative incident in their relation to language. The second writing assignment is to explore their relation to language and writing in the context of their background, taking into account whatever factors seem relevant—age, class, race, ethnic group, sexual politics, region, religion, and so on, as well as gender. We discuss writing blocks, and in the third assignment they write about whatever keeps them from writing or helps them to write, imaging

a muse or an anti-muse. Some of these papers result in dia-
logues as they become conscious of the voices inside them that
embody the struggle to speak or stay silent. Throughout the
course, we read articles and essays from the by now large body
of research and writing on the topic of women and language.
These essays provide models for the students' own writing and
put their struggles with silence and speech into a context.

A 1983 anthology, *Language, Gender and Society*, edited by
Barrie Thorne, Cheris Kramarae and Nancy Henley, contains a
187 page annotated bibliography of work done on women and
language. It seems to me that there are four major types of
research that make up this ocean of work. First is empirical
feminist linguistics in the U.S. and Great Britain which has
focused on 1) speech interactions between women and men—
such as who interrupts whom in conversation, how much air
time people get, who asks more questions, whose conversational topics get picked up, who expresses uncertainty in conversation through the use of tag questions and vague modifiers,
and on 2) the structure of the English language—the effect of
the generic "he" and "man" which make women invisible,
the prevalence of degrading, trivializing and hostile terms for
women available to speakers of English, the custom of women
losing their names as they acquire a husband, the addition of
suffixes such as "ess" and "ette" ("poetess," "suffragette").
The conclusion much of this research leads to is that the sexism encoded in the structure of the language and acted out
in speech situations finally has less to do with gender *per se*
than it does with who has the power to name, to speak, and to
expect that one's words will be heard and valued. As Dale
Spender, a British linguist, says in *Man Made Language*,
women have been a "muted group" (passim).

The second major category of research into women and language has been feminist literary criticism, which has looked:
at the way women writers have been silenced historically; has
uncovered and discovered buried and obscured women writers and is engaged in the task of building a literary history of
women; has discussed the images of women in works by both
male and female writers; has studied the relation between gender, reader, and text; has looked at the forms and genres in

which women writers have expressed themselves; and has barely kept pace with the explosive experimentation in contemporary women's writing.

This renaissance in women's writing is connected to the other two areas of women and language research—the work of the French feminist critics and of women writers writing about their writing process. The French feminist critics, first, connect writing to the body. Hélène Cixous comments: "Woman must write her self: must write about women and bring women to writing, from which they have been driven away as violently as from their bodies" (Marks and de Courtivron, 245). Chantal Chawaf asks,

Isn't the final goal of writing to articulate the body? . . .The novel and its traditional narrative style summarizes, it is a yardstick for measuring distance. But when I write, on the contrary, I move in close and what I see is enormous. I magnify the word with a close-up lens. I examine it at close range: it has its own way of being granulated, ruffled, wrinkled, gnarled, iridescent, sticky. I try to respect its variations in elevation, its sheen, its seeds, and like an artisan I offer them so that they may be touched and eaten. The word must comfort the body. . . .In order to reconnect the book with the body and with pleasure, we must disintellectualize writing" (Marks and de Courtivron, 177).

Madeleine Gagnon grounds her writing in female biological rhythms when she says:

Writing . . . meant erasing as I went along all that had been inscribed on the slate. . . .Learning to exchange blood, milk, tears in the loss of the body, learning to flow, and remembering the traces on the day when they had been erased. . . .I have learned to efface myself a thousand times and each time I return triumphant with pleasure. For me death is daily and monthly, it comes and goes. It doesn't mean *one* unique death to be feared; ever since I started to exist I have been dissolving into all that disappears and comes to life again (Marks and de Courtivron, 179).

The French feminist critics differ from American and British feminist linguists not only in their insistence that language and writing are material and sensual, but also in their attitude

toward silence, which they see not negatively but as a creative
and potentially transformative and revolutionary space. They
agree that women have, historically, been silenced. Xaviere
Gauthier writes:

Women are, in fact, caught in a very real contradiction. Throughout
the course of history, they have been mute, and it is doubtless by virtue of this mutism that men have been able to speak and write. As
long as women remain silent, they will be outside the historical process. But, if they begin to speak and write *as men do*, they will enter
history subdued and alienated; it is a history that, logically speaking,
their speech should disrupt.

   If, however "replete" words (*mots pleins*) belong to men, how can
women speak "otherwise," unless, perhaps we can *make audible* that
which agitates within us, suffers silently in the *holes of discourse*, in
the unsaid, or in the non-sense (Marks and de Courtivron, 162-163).

Julia Kristeva talks of the revolutionary and feminine "moment of rupture and negativity" which "reject[s] everything
finite, definite, structured, loaded with meaning, in the existing state of society" (Marks and de Courtivron, 166, 167).
One needs silence, one needs to listen, in order to connect with
one's creative rhythms. Marguerite Duras writes:

I think "feminine literature" is an organic, translated writing translated from blackness, from darkness. . . .I know that when I write
there is something inside me that stops functioning, something that
becomes silent. I let something take over inside me that probably
flows from femininity. But everything shuts off—the analytic way of
thinking, thinking inculcated by college, studies, reading, experience.
I'm absolutely sure of what I'm telling you now. It's as if I were re-
turning to a wild country (Marks and de Courtivron, 174-175).

   This process of "unnaming," of accepting wildness, absence,
silence as a prelude to new speech, is also the concern of a
number of American women writers writing about the relation
between women and language and about their own writing
process—poet/philosophers Adrienne Rich, Mary Daly, Audre
Lorde, Susan Griffin, Alice Walker, Gloria Anzaldua, Judy
Grahn, and others. Many of these women writers are lesbian,

working class, and/or women of color. Their perspective as doubly or triply outside of a mainstream literary tradition and their use of a language that falsely describes their experience allows them both a dual vision and a radical potential. Mary Daly, in *Gyn/Ecology*, writes: "Overcoming the silencing of women is an extreme act, a sequence of extreme acts. Breaking our silence means living in existential courage. It means discovering our deep sources, our spring" (21). Susan Griffin, in "Thoughts on Writing: A Diary," talks about the voice of the "other" in society and remarks that:

the most interesting creative work is being done at the moment by those who are excluded and have departed from the dominant culture—women, people of color, homosexuals. And this work, unlike the decadent, and abstract, and dadaist, and concrete, and mechanist work of the dominant culture, is not despairing. This work is radiant with will, with the desire to speak; it sings with the clear tones of long suppressed utterance, is brilliant with light, with powerful and graceful forms, with forms that embody feeling and enlarge the capacity of the beholder, of the listener, to feel (116).

She describes her own writing process as the struggle between the voice of despair and the "voice of poetry (joy, playfulness, rebellious vision)." Adrienne Rich talks about the woman writer not as a mystery but prosaically, as "that absorbed, drudging, puzzled, sometimes inspired creature . . . who sits at a desk trying to put words together" (*On Lies*, "'When We Dead Awaken': Writing as Re-Vision," 39) and says that:

if the imagination is to transcend and transform experience it has to question, to challenge, to conceive of alternatives, perhaps to the very life you are living at that moment. You have to be free to play around with the notion that day might be night, love might be hate; nothing can be too sacred for the imagination to turn into its opposite or to call experimentally by another name. For writing is re-naming (43).

The connections between the aesthetic of these writers and the theory of the French feminist writers are apparent. Both expound something that could be called a *feminist erotics of writing*, a writing from the center of oneself, a writing that is sensual rather than abstract, grounded in the world and in the body, creative and revolutionary. Audre Lorde defines it "as an assertion of the life-force of women; of that creative energy empowered, the knowledge and use of which we are not re-claiming in our language, our history, our dancing, our living, our work, our lives" (3-4). She speaks of it as the "capacity for joy" and says: "In touch with the erotic, I become less willing to accept powerlessness, or those other supplied states of being which are not native to me, such as resignation, despair, self-effacement, depression, self-denial" (7).

Perhaps the most useful assignment in the course I teach at the University of Massachusetts/Boston is the writing process paper, in which students are asked to describe in detail *how* they write a paper from the moment they get the assignment until they turn it in, focusing not only on the intellectual pro-cess—how they settle on a thesis, whether they free-write, make outlines, cut and paste, revise six times or not at all—but also on the psychological process of writing—the length and formal variety of their procrastination, where in the pro-cess they block, how and whether they make room in their lives for writing—and the material conditions of their writ-ing—do they need/have a room of their own to write in, do they compose on the typewriter or on legal-sized narrow-ruled pads of paper or, in what will probably be an increasing number of cases, on a word processor, do they take lots of breaks or write in one continuous rush, and so on. One student imaged her writing process as putting a jigsaw puzzle together; another said it was similar to finding an old chair in a garbage pile and slowly and lovingly refinishing it; a third saw it as birthing a child. One woman wrote: "Each time I am assigned a paper I suck in my breath as if I had to move a hundred-pound stone from the entrance to my apartment in order to go on living." Another woman titled her writing process paper "A Journal Record: One Week in the Creation of a Paper" (McDonald, 40). On Monday she said that she had "more or less exhausted the possibilities for meaningful procrastination . . . cleaned the house, baked bread, written letters, taken a sudden interest in learning Russian, created emotional crises around" herself. On Tuesday she sat down in front of the typewriter and blocked, thinking on the one hand, "My mind is an unbreakable pane of glass. It is a telescope to a great spectrum of ideas, a microscope to every mite of detail. . . .The world is open to me. I can write anything!," and on the other hand: "I can't write. My vocabulary has all the flexibility of a marble column and the visionary range of a burrowed mole. . . .My ideas are as profound and original as Ronald Reagan's press conferences." On Wednesday she typed out 79 ideas related to her topic, cut them out with her scissors, placed them in piles, chose one as her main idea, and wrote an outline. On Thursday she faced her writing block again and concluded: "I cannot expect to be able to relax and write this paper when I place in its grips the right to determine my worth as a human being," and, more practically, that in order to write she needed to create a gap in her daily life since "writing doesn't get done between taking out the trash and doing the laundry." Friday she wrote a draft of the paper and for the first time became caught up in the creative joy of it:

This is the part I like best. It's the words that I love. . . .I live in my body more than in my head, and to me words are the sensual aspect of thought. They feel good rolling off the tongue. Their patterns on the page please the eye. They congregate, like old Southern ladies at church, into sentences and paragraphs. The rise and fall of their cadences is punctuated by exclamations (Yes, Jesus!) and commas (MmmHmm), and question marks (Ain't it so?). In their silences, their hushed pauses, a quiet hymn as soft as magnolias rises from their lips.

On Saturday she revised, describing the process as hard work, "almost as difficult as giving up some of my precious rags to Goodwill," feeling un-American as she did away with the more the better, the bigger the better. On Sunday she both loved the paper and hated it. She revised it again. On Monday she neither loved nor hated it, but accepted it, let it go, and turned it in.

While the first decade of feminist language research focused on the power dynamics of language in relation to gender and uncovered what I've come to call a linguistic etiquette of powerlessness, what Robin Lakoff described in negative terms in 1975 as "women's language," attention is now turning to a

positive view of women's language—to the way women write
to each other and to the way we women talk among ourselves.
One of the more interesting chapters of British linguist Dale
Spender's *Man Made Language* is called "Woman Talk," a
study of the mode of discourse of consciousness raising groups.
Another interesting area of research will be, I hope, the modes
of discourse in women's studies classrooms. Three years ago I
had the valuable experience of being a student in a women's
studies classroom when I participated in an NEH Summer
Seminar on Feminism and Modernism. The fifteen high-pow-
ered women in that group who had made it through graduate
school and in most cases into tenure at their colleges and universities had learned, it soon became painfully clear, competitive, hierarchical, linear modes of discourse which ill-suited
the subject matter of the course. We were so relieved to have
found a group that was interested in our feminist thoughts and
analyses of the literature that at first we competed ferociously
for air time, leaving no creative seconds of silence between one
woman's comment and another's; the louder drowned out the
quieter; the faster got to talk more than the slower; we didn't
listen to what anyone was saying because we were each too
busy planning what we were going to say next if we could just
elbow our way into the debate. It was distressing and painful
and ruefully funny when we realized two or three weeks into
the course that it was not enough to have been given the time
—eight weeks in the sunny Sacramento Valley—to talk about
feminist content if we were simply going to replicate the
modes of discourse we had learned in the patriarchal institutions which had trained us, which we all had cogent criticisms
of and in which we were not training others. We worked hard
at learning to slow down, to leave space around each comment,
to really listen to what each person was saying, to build on it
rather than moving right into our own monologues, to allow
everyone air time, and to draw people out and help them develop their ideas. I do not know what the other women got out
of that NEH seminar, but what I learned and relearned about
feminist discourse was at least as important as the opportunity
to practice feminist literary criticism.

In recent feminist literary criticism, attention is beginning to turn toward describing a new and experimental "women's style," as well as looking at the precursors of that style as Gertrude Stein. We are finally being able to answer Virginia Woolf's provocative question, "Is there such a thing as a female sentence?" with a qualified yes.[4] In a paper I presented at the National Women's Studies Association Conference in June, 1984, I talked about the politics of style of twentieth century feminist essayists like Woolf, Meridel LeSueur, and Adrienne Rich, particularly in relation to the tension of writing for more than one audience (Annas, "Style as Politics"). A recent and exciting article by Julia Penelope (Stanley) and Susan J. Wolfe, "Consciousness as Style; Style as Aesthetic" (Thorne, 125-139), looks at the writing of contemporary feminists who are writing primarily for one audience, an audience of women — such writers as Susan Griffin, Mary Daly, Jill Johnston, Kate Millet, Tillie Olsen, and others. Building on Carol Gilligan's work on female moral development, they say that "patriarchal expressive modes reflect an epistemology that perceives the world in terms of categories, dichotomies, roles, stasis, and causation, while female expressive modes reflect an epistemology that perceives the world in terms of ambiguities, pluralities, processes, continuities, and complex relationships" (126). They describe "woman's style" as grounded in "the unrelenting language of process and change" (136):

What is said in one breath may be negated by the succeeding observation. The natural imagery of growth, proliferation, and evolution replaces nature as object and product. Flux is the only experience; stasis is impossible. Labels and abstract nouns as viable perceptive categories give way to active, process verbs and concrete nouns, the language of touch; verbs of specific action replace the abstract, more general verbs. On the discourse level, we find a discursive, conjunctive style instead of the complex, subordinating, linear style of classification and distinction. It is not that there is no classifying taking place, rather that the syntactic structure must accommodate itself to the shifting perspectives of the writer's observing mind. In contrast to a subordinate syntax (in which the complexity of experience is embedded in dependent clauses, reflecting experience already categorized, qualified, detached from its happening), the writer attempts to order her perceptions through a kind of cumulative syntax, using juxtaposed clauses to express the relationships as they suggest themselves. It is the syntax of woman's consciousness. . . . (136-137).

And they say that "the women of the 20th century who write speak out of a tradition of silence, a tradition of the closely guarded, personal, revelatory language of diaries and journals" (125).

At least as important as the production of and experimentation with writing as women is the provision of a space for the writing that is both supportive and constructively critical, that validates where students are in the present as well as urges them to grow and change, that allows them to do the kind of experimental cumulative writing that Julia Penelope and Susan Wolfe describe and also develops the skills of standard expository writing. In the course, students work in supervised dyads and small groups with each other's writing, learning how to give each other suggestions for revision and building critical skills that they will apply, I hope, to their own writing during and after they leave the course. The construction of that kind of nurturing but rigorous/tough space is part of what Adrienne Rich means when she talks about "taking women students seriously" (On Lies, "Taking Women Students Seriously"), properly the subject of another paper, but I do want to point out here the importance of the context in which the work of writing gets done.

Finally, the insights of feminist language research and their application to the teaching of writing are not gender bound, though I have been very grateful to have had the opportunity to work them out with all woman groups during the past three years. I have started structuring writing assignments in introductory writing classes in a way similar to the Writing as Women course, asking men and women students to write about their relation to language and writing in terms of their backgrounds, discussing writing blocks and having them describe their writing processes. A man in one of my introductory writing classes this semester, for example, came up with a very interesting personal insight—he said that as soon as he wrote a really good paragraph, that came out of the center of himself, he promptly blocked. Why, I wonder? Also, I have been trying with some success to replicate modes of feminist discourse in mixed writing classes, training people to listen as well as talk, to take criticism as well as give it, to provide support as well as judgment, to experiment and take risks—overall, to build a writing *community* instead of simply a writing class. Feminist scholarship and pedagogy need to continue to have a separate and uncluttered space of their own in which to work out ideas, and they have also the obligation to—I hate to use jargon, but I will just this once—"mainstream" those ideas and bring them back into the regular classroom where they are desperately needed.

We can find in mythology a rationale for the silencing of women as for so much else. Consider the story of Pandora, the first woman, who was given by the gods in marriage to a mortal man. Invested by the gods with charm, beauty, and a beguiling nature, she was a deceitful gift, a punishment to balance Prometheus' gift of fire to mankind. With her came a jar or box that was not to be opened. Naturally, she opened it. Wouldn't you? According to this patriarchal myth of paradise lost, what flew out were sickness, despair, pain—all the ills that have plagued the world ever since—barely mitigated by hope. In a later version of the myth, the box contained all possible blessings, which escaped the world when the box was opened, leaving only hope.

However, what if we read this myth differently, seeing the contents of the jar as neither good nor evil but simply Pandora's female consciousness—body, soul, and mind—which, placed in a man's world and the institution of marriage, Pandora was to keep repressed, keep the lid on, while the simacrulum of her unawakened self walked benumbed through her husband's palace? Pandora, like Eve and Psyche impelled by a need to know, took off the great lid of the jar with her hands. If we looked at what flew out, not with the frightened and distorting eyes of her husband and the gods as either good or evil, but with new eyes, we might see Pandora releasing women's modes of conceptualization and creativity. In that interpretation, lifting the lid would free Pandora from silence into speech, from ignorance into knowledge, from numbness into feeling, from paralysis into action. It would be a revolutionary act. Certainly in the myth she changed the world by making it more complex.

We are all Pandora, motivated by a need to know our inner and outer worlds when we sit down to write. For when we open the lid, pain does fly out, and anger, fear, and grief—but also joy, and an end to silence.

Notes

1. This poem appears in a slightly different form ("in *her* bottled up is a woman as peppery as curry"—my italics) and as "the woman in the ordinary" in Piercy's book *To Be of Use* (New York: Doubleday, 1973).

2. The general rule I'm following in quoting from student papers is to preserve anonymity unless the paper has been published.

3. From a taped transcript of a class session, Fall 1981.

4. Woolf writes in Chapter 4, "Perhaps the first thing she [the woman writer] would find, setting pen to paper, was that there was no common sentence ready for her use" (132). At the beginning of Chapter 6, she talks about the need for "the development by the average woman of a prose style completely expressive of her mind" (165).

Works Cited

Annas, Pamela J. "Style as Politics/Politics as Style: The Feminist Essay." Paper given at the National Women's Studies Association Conference, June 1983.

Daly, Mary. *Gyn/Ecology. The Metaethics of Radical Feminism.* Boston: The Beacon Press, 1978.

Friedan, Betty. *The Feminist Mystique.* New York: W. W. Norton and Company, Inc., 1963.

Griffin, Susan. "Thoughts on Writing: A Diary." *The Writer on Her Work.* Ed. Janet Sternburg. New York: W. W. Norton and Company, Inc., 1980. 107-120.

Lakoff, Robin. *Language and Woman's Place.* New York: Harper and Row, 1975.

Lorde, Audre. *Uses of the Erotic: The Erotic as Power.* Trumansburg, NY: The Crossing Press, 1978.

McDonald, Karen. "My Writing Process." *Women Studies Quarterly* 12, No. 1 (Spring 1984): 40.

Marks, Elaine and Isabelle de Courtivron, Eds. *New French Feminisms: An Anthology.* Amherst, MA: The University of Massachusetts Press, 1980.

Olsen, Tillie. *Silences.* New York: Delacorte Press/Seymour Lawrence, 1978.

Piercy, Marge. "The Woman in the." *No More Masks: An Anthology of Poems by Women.* Eds. Florence Howe and Ellen Bass. Garden City, NY: Anchor Press/Doubleday Anchor Books, 1973. 247.

Rich, Adrienne. *On Lies, Secrets, and Silence: Selected Prose 1966-1978.* New York: W. W. Norton and Company, 1979.

Spender, Dale. *Man Made Language.* London: Routledge and Kegan Paul, 1980.

Thorne, Barrie, Cheris Kramarae and Nancy Henley, Eds. *Language, Gender and Society.* Rowley, MA: Newbury House Publishers, Inc., 1983.

Woolf, Virginia. *A Room of One's Own.* New York: Harcourt, Brace and Company, 1929.

Women Writing

Wendy Goulston

Whenever I pursue ideas about women in depth, I wonder to what degree and for whom they are true. While skepticism can sharpen understanding, the self-doubt lurking behind my skepticism often blocks my thinking. Theories that suggest that women's socialization produces internalized oppression explain this dilemma: women are often not sure of their own ideas, especially when asked to express them in rhetorical forms that have traditionally been used almost exclusively by men. This is my thesis and my own situation.

Women's traditional sex role socialization, so we read in many studies of sex roles, prepares them to be nurturers, listeners, and assimilators, to trust to other's (male) authority when any important decision or action in the public world is to be made.[1] Thus, women become good in private conversation, especially in the role of empathizing, acknowledging and responding to someone else. Along with this, women are taught to be more concerned with relationship than with logical, conceptual thinking. They are taught the skills and, more deeply, the attitude of pleasing people, rather than of standing up for themselves when it may or may not please others.[2] They are encouraged to develop expertise in the domestic realm, rather than to think and act publicly, yet they learn that society values public contributions more (Chodorow, 173-197).

However limited the truth of these generalizations, they describe norms I learned as I grew up. And other women I speak to say they too feel such pressures in society, from the inside as

well as the outside. I know that I struggle to write in my own
voice and to hone my own thinking, opposed by deeply internalized roles of feminine decorum and compliance. I watch
many (but not all) my adult women students and my friends
grapple with conflicting role pressures as their efforts to develop a public, professional self pull against their sense of obligation to domestic and job responsibilities and constraints.
Learning to speak and to write and in all ways to present oneself as a doer and a thinker in academia and in the labor market
involves for many women a challenge to their very sense of
self.

Unlike most of my students, I came up the traditional academic ladder, encouraged by my parents and teachers to follow
my interests, to press forward in my education. Adept at understanding other people's point of view, quick to appreciate the
aesthetic and epistemological gains of conceptual thinking, I
excelled on paper in spite of my constant sense that everyone knew more than I.

I transferred my private, domestic skills quite effectively to
the classroom, where I could please my (mostly male) professors in the same way I had my father and other teachers, by
grasping and admiring their ideas, interrelating them, fleshing
them out with further examples. Writing papers for professors
was exactly that, and though I agonized over guessing what
was expected and never knew the quality of my work till I
heard the grade, I did get good grades, which bewildered and
pleased me. My essays were rich with what I had learned of
other periods, other cultures, others' minds. Though I had
many questions, it never occurred to me to use them to speculate about other, more provocative theories. I did not dream of
challenging what I was taught. That would have been painfully
unwomanly. As many other female academics have remarked,
I never noticed that I read virtually no women writers, or that
women's experience was so undervalued as to be missing from
my curriculum.[3] I kept away from subjects like political science, mathematics, the hard sciences, where "the real world"
seemed to lurk. I dreaded competing with men, avoided publicly pitting myself against anyone. Academia felt safe: I enjoyed studying and knew how to pass exams, while pretending

to know very little. (Everyone hated a "brain," especially a female one). I was afraid of the big dangerous world, where one needed political awareness and insensitivity to not being liked, assertive initiative and the ability to act on one's knowledge.

No one, from the time I entered Sydney University, aged sixteen, through two years graduate study in Oxford and one year at the Hebrew University, Jerusalem, wanted to know how I proposed to use this knowledge to earn my living. Until I finished my doctorate, aged thirty, at the American University in Washington, D. C., I myself never had the courage to face that question. I wanted to believe that as long as I kept pleasing (male) authorities by doing well in my studies and looking after my friends and family emotionally, somehow the future would unfold "as it should." I relied heavily on my mother's philosophy that a young woman should study and train till she had a husband to look after her, in case he died one day and left her to support her children.

It was not until I came, newly married, to America, and entered a doctoral program with women professors and students who were feminists, that it dawned on me that I didn't know what I really wanted to learn. I was accustomed to being told what approach to take. Paradoxically, I was already a teacher that students saw as an authority figure; I had developed a nontraditional teaching style and philosophy based on helping students in their own struggle to define and to develop their interests. Yet when it came to my own writing, I was unable to strike out my pattern of thought. A doctoral professor who was also my friend gave me the first comment I had ever received about the structure of my paragraphs: "Wendy, why do you bury your topic sentences in the middle of your paragraphs?" I started seeing: my dense sentences subtly hid their conceptual framework in a luxuriance of insightful detail. Forcing the main ideas out in the open made me feel exposed, afflicted me with mental paralysis. I know now that for me and for many women, learning to write as a strong-voiced, confident individual uncomfortably jolts one's sense of self and one's female stereotype; it involves more than simply learning writing skills.

Writing, as it has been traditionally required in college, can be understood as a "male" or establishment form, in as much as the aims and modes of scientific, informative, exploratory, and persuasive discourse, even, until recently, literary discourse, have been defined and developed by men heading intellectual institutions, and by the predominantly male writers whose ideas the professors have valued. College writing trained and still does train students to use their minds in time-hallowed ways. For female students this still, I suspect, means straining to attain a style, voice and role that is hard to integrate with sexual and domestic success. Although the woman who excels at school learns to write pleasing papers for professors, she does not write them from her whole "center." When she leaves the security of the assigned essay, or when she experiences critical analysis as alien, her vulnerability, anger and uncertainty restrain her pen.

I am solving my own "public" writing dilemma by applying and discussing various streams of feminist thought in literature, psychology, sociology and philosophy, as well as by seeing my own teaching and learning style affirmed in new theory and methods of teaching writing. It seems to me that we can draw on all that illuminates women's experience to help ourselves and our students develop stronger voices. Ideally, women in writing classes (or women having trouble writing strongly in any class) would read some of the fine literary works by and about women and together relate the female characters' experiences to their own experiences speaking and writing.[4]

They would for example, discuss western love poetry in the light of Simone de Beauvoir's *The Second Sex*, examining her perception that women find their sense of themselves as "subject" undermined at puberty, when their new sexuality disturbingly defines them as "object." They would think about how such a change might be related to confidence in their own ideas and in their ability to argue them forcibly. Students would read Agnes Smedley's *Daughter of Earth* with Virginia Woolf's *A Room of One's Own* and Tillie Olsen's *Silences*, to learn how women have been prevented from developing and expressing themselves. They would discuss and write about their knowledge, responding to Adrienne Rich's experience of an imagination shackled by traditional roles, and her poetry and prose's call for revision. Writing classes would read Carol Gilligan's *In a Different Voice*, and question the implications of her ideas for women learning to write self-reliantly. They would think about Gilligan's idea that women seem to develop an ethics different from men's, one that is based on caring rather than on rules, an ethics learned through empathy and attachment rather than through achievement and separation. Alice Walker's novels would expand and enrich their discussion. Doris Lessing's novels and Nancy Chodorow's and Elizabeth Janeway's psychology and sociology would be standard reading, providing insight into our culture's social mythology that pressures woman to stay in her publicly silent, child-centered place in a man's world. And students would judge the personal relevance of Rita Weathersby's findings that more adult women than men see their educational experiences as a support for a life transition, which means that women students experience college differently from men and use it differently. Such discussions enable women to consider how gender has influenced their self development and education, freeing them of depressingly limited misconceptions about their own abilities, supportively inviting them to try out, in a college essay, the ideas and feelings they have protectively, quietly harbored. By explaining to other women the main ideas and personal relevance of these readings, students (and their professors) can strengthen their exposition and analysis skills in deeply empowering ways.

Needless to say, few writing classes do currently help students understand how their writing difficulties connect with their sense of who they are and whom they are writing for. While a small number of women professors and their students are working on writing problems in relation to gender, most college faculty and students regard writing problems as simply a lack of editing skills or of talent.[5] More recently, racial and cultural barriers to "establishment" writing have been better recognized,[6] though women's particular experience has not been explicitly examined and applied to mainstream writing pedagogy.

In the last fifteen years, however, a revolution has been slowly occurring in pedagogical writing theory, producing new

research and teaching methods that seem much better suited
to the needs of women. Not surprisingly, women, for the first
time, have influenced and contributed significantly to the
change of perspective. Traditionally, students have been
taught the *rules* of writing and papers have been *corrected*
when handed in for a grade at the end of the course. Written
work, seen as a final product, has shown whether one has
passed or failed in doing the professor's bidding. Papers have
come back ribboned with a "good," or scarred with red marks,
grammatical errors underlined and "so what?" branding margins. This approach to teaching writing does not teach students how to increase the clarity and force of their own writing
voice.

Though many professors (in all fields) still "teach" this way,
those that know about current research and thinking by Linda
Flower, Ann Berthoff, James Britton, Peter Elbow, Janet Emig,
Nancy Sommers, Kenneth Bruffee and others help students
focus non-judgmentally on the process of writing and rewriting, rather than criticizing one final product.[7] They do not criticize at all, but rather "listen" to the writer in a believing rather
than an attacking stance, encouraging her to keep reshaping
what she has to say until a reader can clearly understand it.
The revising process is open for discussion.

This new emphasis on revision and positive attitude toward
teaching writing has been influenced by Sommers' (1980) research on the ways strong writers and "inexperienced" writers
write. Experienced writers usually begin, like inexperienced
writers, by spewing out their messy, rich concoction of ideas,
but they do so with more gusto, usually with less self-criticism
and despair. Experienced writers expect to write many drafts
before their focus becomes sharp, their ideas shaped, their sentences vital. Inexperienced writers, hampered by trying to produce "what is expected" quickly, look at their first drafts as
failures. They think "good writers" create good prose fast and
effortlessly. Inexperienced writers labor over their second
drafts, correcting spelling and grammatical errors, not knowing
how to take their ideas further, not explaining or illustrating so
a reader will understand. Rather, they think they have already
done their best to "put their thoughts on paper." They are not

accustomed to rereading their writing from the reader's perspective. Indeed, if they are women socialized as I and many of us are, they find the male professor's perspective a threatening one to adopt toward their own work. They depend heavily from the start on the academic models they have seen or imagined, and struggle self-doubtingly to produce what they guess will please his all-knowing, all-judging eyes. They feel reassured, but still puzzled and insecure if they are told the work is good, and hopeless or rebellious if it is judged weak.

Interestingly, the new approaches to teaching writing adopt a position and utilize skills that have traditionally been associated with female style. They contrast with the rhetorical professorial academic stance of the past. The new teachers' and fellow students' role in aiding students to write well is not to "profess" and pass judgment, but to question and to wish to understand. Assuming that the writer can surface and clarify her thought, the instructor encourages her to collaborate with other students to keep developing her ideas. Because it assumes that the writer has something valuable to say, this teaching method provides the respect and nurturing support that women students especially need.

As teachers and researchers increasingly demystify the writing process, they are teaching students to learn from each other when reading and commenting on each other's writing, so the teacher is not the sole reader and arbiter; students are learning not to be devastated by criticism that supports and furthers their self expression. Thus, teachers encourage students' prewriting, writing, and rewriting. They thereby help students integrate and affirm their private and public sense of self, because revision transforms first draft, writer-based (private) prose to reader-based (public) final drafts. Prewriting is, after all, what women have been doing for centuries in letters and journals and conversations with each other, "free writing," brainstorming, meditating, overflowing with uncensored feelings and ideas. Using these familiar, expressive modes as a basis for academic writing, benefiting from the caring attention and listening skills of writing center, tutors and professors, learning traditional rhetorical theory in a context that acknowledges women's exclusion from that tradition, women can draw on their own thinking and feeling to develop the rhetorical strategies that best suit their styles, their arguments, their values.

If this new approach to writing were to be limited to writing classes, while traditional approaches continued in other classes, much would be lost. Luckily, another advance in the teaching of writing has forced professors in all fields, at some universities, to take a new look at how they use writing in their work with students. Increasingly, the teaching of writing is moving "across the curriculum." Administration and faculty are realizing that writing is not separate from thinking: rather, it is one of the best tools for exploring and analyzing ideas, an intrinsic part of learning any conceptual subject matter. So faculty in all disciplines (at many schools) are being trained in the new approaches to writing. Unfortunately, many teachers, in all fields, insist on teaching as they have always done, asking for term papers they then judge, not helping the student, from the beginning, to develop her ideas on paper (Hairston, 1983-84). Many professors, on the other hand, are changing their approach now that they better understand that many students experience traditional academic language conventions as alien. The latter are structuring sequenced writing assignments that help students move from experience to abstraction to an integration of the two through several drafts during a course of study.

Professors who heed William Perry's *Forms of Intellectual and Ethical Development in the College Years* comprehend that academic ideas, and the forms in which they are communicated, often affront the student's sense of truth and value. While their sex role socialization may prepare women to grasp and adopt the points of view that please professors, many women students feel impostors in their knowledge and in their adoption of rhetorical forms. Yet exposing and developing their own thought feels dangerous and requires ongoing support. When professors have the openness, flexibility and respect to include texts by and about women, to adopt the new approaches to writing and to help students to value and explain their own experience in relation to ideas, there will be more chance for women to find out what they have to say and to say it powerfully.

Notes

1. For example Kay Deaux, *Behavior of Women and Men* (Monterey, CA: Brooks/Cole, 1976); Dorothy Dinnerstein, *The Mermaid and the Minotaur: Sexual Arrangements and Human Malaise* (New York: Harper and Row, 1976); Elizabeth Janeway, *Man's World, Woman's Place: A Study in Social Mythology* (New York: William Morrow, 1971); Virginia O'Leary, *Toward Understanding Woman* (Monterey, CA: Brooks/Cole, 1977); E. A. Erikson, in "Womanhood and Inner Space" (1968), reprinted in J. Strouse, Ed. *Women and Analysis* (New York: Dell, 1976) argues that women's role has a physical basis. Contrast his argument with that of Luise Eichenbaum and Susie Orbach, in *Understanding Women: A Feminist Psychoanalytic Approach* (New York: Basic Books, Inc., 1983).

2. See Carol Gilligan, *In a Different Voice: Psychological Theory and Women's Development* (Cambridge, MA: Harvard University Press, 1982).

3. See, for instance, Florence Howe, "A Report on Women and the Profession," *College English* 32 (May 1971): 817-854, and Elaine Showalter, "Women and the Literary Curriculum," *College English* 32 (May, 1971): 855-862, and Adrienne Rich, "'When We Dead Awaken:' Writing as Revision," in *On Lies, Secrets, and Silence: Selected Prose 1966-1978* (New York: Norton, 1979) 35-49. For more recent discussions of feminist influences on the curriculum, see *A Feminist Perspective in the Academy, The Difference It Makes*, Eds. Elizabeth Langland and Walter Grove (Chicago: University of Chicago Press, 1981).

4. A few academic writing teachers are already seeing the importance of linking writing instruction to how the woman student understands her experience and heritage as a woman in a patriarchal world. See Florence Howe, "Identity and Expression: A Writing Course for Women," *College English* 32 (May, 1971): 863-871 and Pamela Annas, "Writing As Women," *Women's Studies Quarterly* (Spring, 1984): 38-39. Faculty at The Education For Women's Development Project,

Rockland Community College, are also researching and teaching women about the problems women encounter in gaining a sense of voice; such work has direct implications for women writing.

5. Maxine Hairston discusses traditional and new attitudes toward teaching writing in "The Winds of Change: Thomas Kuhn and the Revolution in the Teaching of Writing," in *Writing Across the Curriculum, Current Issues in Higher Education* 3 (1983-84): 4-10.

6. See especially Mina P. Shaughnessy's *Errors and Expectations: A Guide for the Teacher of Basic Writing* (New York: Oxford University Press, 1977), a seminal work on writing problems associated with the educationally deprived.

7. See, for instance, Ann Berthoff, "From Problem-Solving to a Theory of Imagination," *College English* 33 (March 1972): 636-649; James Britton et al, *The Development of Writing Abilities*, 11-18, MacMillan Research Series (London: MacMillan Education, 1975); Kenneth Bruffee, "The Brooklyn Plan: Attaining Intellectual Growth through Peer-Group Tutoring," *Liberal Education* 61, No. 4 (December 1978): 447-468; Peter Elbow, *Writing With Power: Techniques for Mastering the Writing Process* (New York: Oxford University Press, 1981); Janet Emig, "Writing As a Mode of Learning," *College Composition and Communication* 28 (May 1977): 122-128; Linda S. Flower, *Problem Solving Strategies for Writing* (New York: Harcourt Brace Jovanovich, 1981); Nancy Sommers, "Revision Strategies of Student Writers and Experienced Writers," *College Composition and Communication* 31 (December 1980): 378-388.

Works Cited

Chodorow, Nancy. "Being and Doing: A Cross-Cultural Examination of the Socialization of Males and Females." *Woman in Sexist Society: Studies in Power and Powerlessness.* Eds. Vivian Gornick and Barbara K. Moran. New York: Basic Books, Inc., 1971. 173-197.

Perry, William G. *Forms of Intellectual and Ethical Development in the College Years.* New York: Holt, Rinehart and Winston, Inc., 1970.

Rich Adrienne. *Diving Into the Wreck: Poems 1971-1972.* New York: W. W. Norton and Company, Inc., 1973.

Weathersby, Ritz Preszler. "Education for Adult Development: The Components of Qualitative Change." *New Directions for Higher Education: Vol. 29, Educating Learners of All Ages.* Eds. Elinor Greenburg, et. al. San Francisco: Jossey-Bass, Inc., Publishers, 1980. 9-22.

The Sexual Politics of the One-To-One Tutorial Approach and Collaborative Learning

Carol A. Stanger

How does a feminist teach writing? For my purposes, a broad definition of *feminist* will suffice: a person concerned with understanding and lessening in some way the sexism, patriarchy and male superiority in our society. If we accept the idea that the classroom is a microcosm of our society and that teaching is a political act, then this definition would satisfy those feminists who are political activists as well as those who are not.

"How does a feminist teach writing?" can be recast as another question: which, if any, teaching approach to writing treats men and women equally in the classroom? In this connection, other questions present themselves. What are the sexual politics created by a particular pedagogical approach? Do these politics match or change those of the society outside the classroom? Do the language, genres, and other elements of expression valued in the classroom favor one sex over another?

I deliberately address the teaching of writing in particular. There is a compelling reason why. When one begins to read in the field of women's studies, one quickly discovers a recurring theme: throughout history and until about a hundred years ago, almost all women have been deprived of their "voice" as thinkers and as writers. Verena Tarrant's fate in *The Bostonians* symbolizes this situation. Even the fact that, unlike most women, she has a little education and a record of success as a speaker cannot save her. On the eve of her most important public speech, she is rendered mute by Basil Ransom's presence. He wraps her in a cape, which makes her anonymous, and takes her away from a public life into a private one. Such a life requires neither serious thinking nor writing.

Many critical and historical feminist studies deal with the silencing of women like Verena under patriarchy. In *In A Different Voice*, Carol Gilligan describes the silencing of the female personality when distorted under traditional, male-centered theories of moral development. In *The Madwoman in the Attic*, Sandra Gilbert and Susan Gubar show how the woman artist of the nineteenth century was trapped in male literary constructs, her situation described powerfully in images of physical and mental confinement. In *The Voyage In*, Elizabeth Abel, Marianne Hirsh, and Elizabeth Langland point out the frequent failed self-realization of women in the novel of female development. It is important to point out, nevertheless, that all of these works stress female accomplishment against considerable odds. For example, Gilbert and Gubar deal with Emily Dickinson in a chapter called "Strength in Agony." Still, each book does record a history of silencing and the fact that many women who managed to write never reached their full potential because their energies were drawn off by husbands, fathers, children, and a patriarchal literary tradition (see Elaine Showalter's, *A Literature of Their Own*); it is important for teachers today to create the conditions for female students to write—to give Verena back her voice and her podium.

When I say it is important to help female students write, I am making an assumption about language and its gender that I cannot take for granted. It is that language is a cultural artifact but that it is not a sex-neutral one. Depending on the sex of the speaker, it has either a male gender or a female one. I am arguing that Eve can name as well as Adam, if she can be taught not to speak "as a man." (I will demonstrate how this can occur later in the paper.)

Thus I am arguing that language is not always male-dominated as Mary Daly claims. It is not always inadequate because it is only "men's" language, thus incomplete, as the French feminists argue. Hélène Cixous, Luce Irigaray, and Marguerite Duras, as Adrienne Munich writes, "ascribe a male gender to language and find the feminist at the level of the silent, the unconscious. Discourse—linear, logical, and theoretical—is masculine. When women speak, therefore, they cannot help but enter male-dominated discourse; speaking women are silent as women" (2).

It may be true that certain elements of discourse, such as straightness, logic, and a pull towards the theoretical are often found in the literature of the French male; I do not know enough French literature to say. But the presence of a linear quality, logic, and a theoretical bent in English, Irish, and American literature written by men needs to be further explored. Even the premier male text, *Paradise Lost*, can hardly be described as linear. Some of Yeats' poetry (for example, the Byzantium poems) can hardly be described as logical, nor does Faulkner's fiction value the theoretical over the concrete. For instance, the reader recalls the details of the bedroom scene in "A Rose for Emily" rather than Faulkner's ideas. In general, the ideas of a good fiction writer are embedded in a metaphor or situation. Further, when we consider the work of male writers from other cultures, such as the Mexican surrealist, Carlos Fuentes, it becomes clear that Cixous, Irigaray and Duras are overgeneralizing when they consider all masculine discourse linear, logical and theoretical. Either they are being ethnocentric or they do not intend their assertions about discourse to be applied to other cultures.

What is more, to accept silence as the female linguistic position seems to me to yield the culture's language to males too quickly. Munich says in the quote above, "speaking women are silent as women." Her statement reminds me of an inn in New England called The Silent Woman, a reflection of a type which dates at least as far back as the *New Testament*, a type forged by a misogynistic vision. Of course, the French feminists understand this and enjoy the irony of turning a male image back on itself. Writers like Isak Dinesen, for example, in her short story "The Blank Page" have shown that silence can speak, that a blank page of linen in a convent can tell a story of female escape from a patriarchal sexual economy.

Asking if there is a written language of female gender does not undercut this unspoken language or silent female expression in ritual and art. Feminist historian Gerda Lerner asserts that "It is important to understand that 'women's culture' is

not and should not be seen as a subculture. It is hardly possible
for the majority to live in a subculture. . . .Women live a
duality—as members of the general culture and as partakers of
women's culture" (199). On the other hand, anthropologists
Shirley and Edwin Ardener suggest that "women constitute a
muted group, the boundaries of whose culture and reality over-
lap, but are not wholly contained by, the *dominant (male)
group* [italics hers]." By the term "muted," Ardener suggests

problems both of language and of power. Both muted and dominant
groups generate beliefs or order ideas of social reality at the unconscious level, but dominant groups control the forms or structures in
which consciousness can be articulated. Thus muted groups must me-
diate their beliefs through the allowable forms of dominant structures. Another way of putting this would be to say that all language is
the language of the dominant order, and women, if they speak at all,
must speak through it (199-200).

But since in terms of numbers, if not in terms of power, women
are a dominant culture, is it not possible that *under the right
conditions* women's beliefs can find expression in language,
even if they have not often done so in the past?

Once a teacher recognizes that there is a history of potential
female writers who have been excluded from the literary conversation, he or she must encourage female students to write.
How does he or she accomplish this? And, given that language
can have a female gender, how does he or she create the conditions to generate "women's language"?

To answer her questions, this concerned teacher might consider two major approaches used in the teaching of composition: (1) the one-to-one tutorial and (2) collaborative learning.
The first approach, the one-to-one tutorial, was developed
by the late Roger H. Garrison at Westbrook College. This approach is widely used in colleges and high schools across the
country. The Garrison approach is based on the belief that the
problem in teaching writing is to find ways to keep students
writing all the time and to provide constant and almost immediate feedback for the writer from the instructor. Thus, students are given a string of assignments, and they meet with

their editor-on-the-spot, their writing teacher, for feedback during different stages of writing a paper. Such feedback is important because the Garrison approach assumes that the major training device in learning how to write is *rewriting*. Theoretically, at least, as students meet with their editor again and again, they learn how to diagnose their own writing difficulties and how to resolve them—that is, how to rewrite effectively. Consequently, they become less and less dependent on the instructor.

Let me illustrate the one-to-one tutorial with a typical Westbrook student, for example, a female student in the nursing program. This student, Marie, has written a persuasion paper on abortion; she is in the first draft stage. In this situation, her audience is clearly her teacher, not the other students in the class, her peers. After the student before her is finished, Marie comes up with a paper. Notice that the instructor doesn't consider his or her thirty students as a group, a class; instead, they are only thirty individuals. (It is simply out of administrative convenience that the students meet as a group; recognizing this, some instructors who use the approach cancel classes and make a series of individual appointments instead.) In the Garrison approach the relationship is between the teacher and each individual student, not between or among students. The members of the class are not encouraged to read one another's work; all work on their own writing while they wait to see the teacher.

Marie sits down next to the instructor and hands him or her her paper. If he or she is a good editor, that is, a good listener, a fast reader, a good diagnostician, he or she will offer criticism which is carefully worded such as, "You have an excellent thesis, but your organization is unclear. Fix it and then see me." Assuming that the class has covered organization, the student may go back to her desk and reorganize her paper. It is equally likely that she may ask the instructor for further explanation and more suggestions. In that case, he or she may say, "What's confusing is that you put your most important reason first instead of last," and show her two ways she might reorganize the paper, such as Nestorian order or the concession form.

Students like Marie often ask for more help from the teacher
although the Garrison method claims to make the student less
dependent. This is because the structure of the student-teacher
relationship in the Garrison approach is the traditional hierarchical one. In fact, it is modeled on the apprentice writer-editor
relationship that Garrison learned when he was a professional
writer.

The student-teacher relationship is hierarchical in a number
of ways. Implied in the idea of working with an editor is that
he or she has plenty of models in mind. (In contrast, most peer
critics have not been sufficiently exposed to models to call
them immediately to mind.) Knowledge of these models gives
authority to the editor's response. Models express the male
value of the ideal text; the ideal text is a male value because it
expresses hierarchical thinking and absolute external values.
Cynthia Caywood and Gillian Overing make this point in their
article included in this anthology, "Writing Across the Curriculum: A Model for a Workshop and a Call for Change." In the
case of Marie's paper, it would be instructive to consider
whether the essay was simply disorganized or whether the paper was organized in a more organic, female form which was
lost on a male reader expecting to see Nestorian order, a male
model. Implied in the concept of the ideal text is that an author
or reader can own or control a text. When Marie gives her paper
to her teacher, her writing is no longer hers; the writer has no
authority. In other words which of the different possibilities
latent in her first draft she wants to say no longer matters; it
is only the reading given by this member of the phallocentric
community that counts. (When a female teacher uses an ideal
text, she reads "like a man.") As Sandra Gilbert and Susan Gubar point out, in *The Madwoman in the Attic*, bestowing authority on a piece of writing and controlling an interpretation
are all patriarchal notions (4-5). So, in the one-to-one tutorial,
the instructor judges the paper against an ideal text, a compos-
ite of the male canon, and bestows authority on the essay as
well as controlling its interpretation. Sensing this political reality, how would Marie feel empowered to revise on her own?
So, in the writing classroom using the one-to-one tutorial, we

find an illustration of the Ardeners' ideas of how female language must filter through the dominant culture, represented by the teacher. Marie's ideas, patterns of thought, and diction are forced through a screen of the dominant culture.

The second approach currently used in the teaching of composition is collaborative learning. I am referring to the method of collaborative learning developed by Kenneth A. Bruffee. Although the terms collaborative learning and group work are sometimes used interchangeably, even by experienced practitioners of collaborative learning, there are some significant differences which help to set collaborative learning apart from ordinary group work as used in most classrooms. First, students in a group are only engaged in collaborative learning if the goal of the task is the learning of high-level critical thinking skills. These are interpretation, application, analysis, synthesis and evaluation. In contrast, students in a group are only engaged in ordinary group work if the goal of the task is the learning of low-level critical thinking skills. These are memorization and straight-forward translation.

Second, students in a group are only engaged in collaborative learning when the task asks questions that have more than one answer or, better yet, are controversial. In a literature class such a question might be: "In *Moby Dick* what does the whiteness of the whale symbolize?" This is a good question because there is genuine disagreement among literary critics over its answer.[1] In contrast, a less productive question for collaborative learning might be, "What is the setting of the beginning of *Moby Dick*?" This is a poor question for group work because the teacher has the "right answer" in his or her head and is waiting to see if the group can guess what it is.

In the 1950's the basic idea of collaborative learning was first developed by a group of British secondary school teachers and by a biologist studying British post-graduate medical education. Since 1952 collaborative learning, as a pedagogical approach for teaching composition and literature, has been highly developed in America by Bruffee and the Fellows of the Brooklyn College Institute in Training Peer Tutors and the Asnuntuck Community College Institute in Collaborative

Learning. At present, this approach is probably less widely used in colleges across the country than the one-to-one tutorial approach.

Collaborative learning is based on the belief that writing (and thinking) is naturally a social act. For example, professional writers and scholars almost routinely share their work. However, English teachers who may share each stage of their manuscripts with members of writers' groups are likely to teach their composition students to write through the one-to-one tutorial between teacher and student. In contrast, collaborative learning mobilizes the students themselves to enhance each others' intellectual growth. Collaborative learning replaces the artificiality of the traditional situation, where the students write exclusively for the teacher, with something that makes more sense—writing for the peer group. A student's instructor is not an ideal audience for a student's writing. First, the student's content, while thoughtful for his or her stage of development, is frequently distant from the concerns of the instructor. Second, the student's language is almost always not the instructor's. And third, most students correctly sense the temporariness and artificiality of an academic audience.

In contrast, peer critics tend to have more in common with students in their use of the elements of writing. First, the writer's content is usually close to the concerns of the critic since they are the same age. Second, the writer's language is almost always close to the critic's since they are both undergraduates. And third, the writer correctly perceives that this audience is "the real thing." Further, he or she understands that it is not a temporary audience; this is because beyond the semester, he or she will continue to care deeply about what his or her contemporaries think of him or her. In sum, student writer and peer critic create a more natural and realistic writing situation.

As Kenneth Bruffee puts it,

... the writing which students do as peer critics tends to be the most "real" writing they ever do in college. The task is clear-cut and unequivocal. The audience [the peer critic] is [immediately at] hand and deeply interested. The effect of this immediacy is that students who have never learned, or never bothered, to write with care, learn in a hurry as peer critics, because the feedback from what they write is strongly reinforced by the peer influence of the increasingly tight-knit intellectual community of the class (459).

Thus, in collaborative learning the problem in teaching writing is how to marshal the influence of the peer group, the single most powerful force in undergraduate education, so that students can teach themselves and their classmates. In a collaborative learning class there is less direct teaching, but there is much more learning. In fact, teaching becomes a process of creating conditions in which collaborative learning can occur. If students are to teach themselves and their classmates, then the problem is how to get students to talk about writing with one another as well as with the teacher. The issues of feedback (one kind of talk about writing) and constant rewriting, which Garrison considers important, are also considered important by Bruffee and the community of teachers who practice his brand of collaborative learning. But, in collaborative learning, feedback and revision have a different and more powerful impetus than they do in the one-to-one tutorial approach. This impetus is peer-group influence. When writing is a social act, it is natural to ask for criticism and to rewrite to satisfy an audience of peers.

With this introduction to collaborative learning in mind, consider this illustration. For the sake of the clearest comparison of the two teaching approaches, I will again use Marie and her persuasion paper on abortion. This time she is having trouble deciding if her paper has a proposition that fits, and she has asked her instructor for help. With Marie's permission, her instructor has duplicated her essay and distributed it to the class. Students have been divided into heterogeneous groups of five or six; each group has a mixture of sexes, ethnic and racial groups, and personalities. The task of all the groups is to answer the question, what is the proposition of this paper? (This is a real question, because the paper has a lot of internal problems which prevent a quick answer by the instructor.) Before the groups answer that question, they have been asked only to summarize the three paragraphs of the author's paper. In other

words, they have been asked to paraphrase what each paragraph says. They have also been asked to explain how each
paragraph functions, what it does, for example, "gives a first
reason for the proposition." In each group, a recorder has been
selected to summarize the discussion. Then each group is
asked to come to a consensus. If there is disagreement among
one or two members of the group, this disagreement is noted in
the recorder's report. However, if there is widespread disagreement, the consensus is that the group agrees to disagree. After
the teacher gives the group its instructions and before the
task begins, Marie is asked to read the paper to the class. The
teacher does not keep the author anonymous, as teachers often
do, because he or she believes that writing is a social act, and
students do not own their words unless they share them. Marie
has read her work to her peers all semester, so she is fairly
comfortable reading it now.

The group begins its task. Rather than being five individuals,
each of whom works only with the teacher, the members of
the group become a collectivity. The strongest individualists
may merge less than the other group members, but everyone in
the group is pulled in as the group comes to take on a life of its
own. It is this sense of transcendence of one's individuality
that produces the oceanic feeling that is the powerful unconscious attraction of small group work. In *The Reproduction of
Mothering*, psychoanalytic critic Nancy Chodorow explains
the root of this attraction by calling attention to the preoedipal
stage of female development. Both preoedipal boys and girls
have a perfect sense of oneness with the mother, a primary in-
timacy. Chodorow says that boys are forced to renounce such
primary love and primary identification in order to resolve the
Oedipal complex, while girls are forced to circumscribe primary love and primary identification in order to have any identity distinct from the mother's. She claims that most people
who have experienced this oceanic feeling want to recreate this
experience and most people try to do so (78-79). Marriage or
parenting can provide this experience. Successful collaboration
in the classroom also provides this experience, however brief.
In the sense that collaborative learning taps learners' early experiences with their mothers, it is a feminist pedagogy.

At the next point in the collaborative task, our cultural training helps move the group to consensus. What helps bring consensus about is not only the intellectual weight of each participant's argument, but the negotiation between men and women. More specifically, it is the negotiation between male and female moral values, which reflect gender differences. I base this statement on the recent work of a feminist psychologist Carol Gilligan. In her book, *In A Different Voice*, she argues that men tend to value individualism and abstractions, such as rights; in contrast, women tend to value connectedness to others and think about abstractions, such as rights, in terms of the human cost involved in upholding them. Gilligan says that most men think in terms of a hierarchy of right and wrong, a ladder, whereas women tend to think in terms of a network of human relationships, a web.

Gilligan's ideas can be applied to a group reaching consensus under a time pressure. If I were to research these ideas, a principal hypothesis would be that most male students tend to protect their individual opinions and fight for the answer that's "right," whereas most female students push for compromise, even at the expense of forwarding their own opinions, so that the ideas of everyone in the group are included and nobody is left out. The cultural context, how men and women are socialized into holding different, but equally valid, moral values, is what makes collaboration work.

When such a group reaches consensus, what exactly has been negotiated among the members of the group? In this particular task, they have been asked to do a descriptive outline of Marie's paper and agree upon a recorder's report that answers the question, does her paper have a thesis? In effect, what this task asks them to do is to negotiate a language. For example, a female member of a group may not agree with a male member that Marie's second paragraph "gives a first reason for the proposition." Instead she may argue that the second paragraph "opposes the proposition and then refutes opposition." Or, she may agree with the male student about the paragraph's function, but find his wording unacceptable. Although Gilligan's ideas would make one expect that female students usually push for compromise, it is not always the case. I have seen many groups where women push for what is right or dominate the group with their ideas, and where men think of the group task in human terms. (I must admit, however, that more men than women fit Gilligan's pattern.) People in groups do not always fit Gilligan's types because of the number of variables besides sex found in group composition: race, religion, and personality.

All these variables come into play when men and women in a collaborative learning group negotiate a language for the recorder's report to be shared with the rest of the class. What is happening during a collaborative task is a dialogue between men's and women's language. Although we would expect that male language would dominate, the new social structure of the peer learning group, the lack of a patriarchal presence "teaching," and the presence of strong and vocal women in the group can combine to give women's language the power to surface and replace men's language. In a group with more women than men, it is possible that women's language would become the language of the dominant order, and that men's language would have to speak through it, like a white musician playing jazz. It is also possible that, whatever the social structure, female students in academia will cross-dress in men's language because female students have been conditioned to do so. So, without further inquiry, I cannot say with certainty that collaborative learning will help Marie write like a woman and will help her peer respond to Marie's paper like a woman, but I would argue for its possibility.

Once consensus has been reached within a group, this consensus is reported to the other groups by the recorders. With the teacher's help, all the groups work towards a new consensus. Hopefully, this new consensus will be composed of women's language as well as men's. Still the consensus of all the students in the class is not the last word; it does not have final authority. The class must test its answers against the teacher's. He or she has authority as a representative of a larger knowledge community. So the entire class and the teacher negotiate the answer or answers to the question raised—that is, together they create the knowledge that is learned during the session. Knowledge, in this context, is not being defined as "fact" handed down by an authority figure; instead, it is something fluid that the group and the teacher create during their interaction. In other words, knowledge is a social artifact in a collaborative class; thereby, in a meaningful way, there is no hierarchy in a collaborative class. The writing teacher who uses collaborative learning, such as small group or peer criticism, values a lack of hierarchical structure in the student-teacher relationship. For example, in the group work just described, the power relationship among the teacher and his or her students is different from the traditional relationship. Power does not stay with the teacher. On the contrary, power flows from the teacher to everyone in the room, and then from student to student. Or, for instance, when one teaches writing using peer criticism, the lack of hierarchy is evident in the use of writing for the peer group. The assumption behind peer criticism is that the teacher is not the only source of help for rewriting, that students can give valuable feedback to one another. Small group work and peer criticism create an alternative social structure in the classroom.

An objection might be raised that the alternative structure is not non-hierarchical because the teacher is not a peer in terms of his or her knowledge about writing. It is true that the instructor who uses group work has an undeniable core of authority stemming from membership in the knowledge communities of writers and English teachers. It would be dishonest to deny this. Yet, in spite of this core of authority, there is no recourse to a single authority in a collaborative class. Instead, authority comes from a consensus among the groups and the teacher, the representative of a larger knowledge community.

Let me return to my initial question. How does a feminist teach writing? I hope this discussion has shown the need to recast the question this way: how does a feminist create the conditions for students to learn? If Marie could speak to her prototype, Verena, she would say (in women's language, I hope) that more learning can take place in the relationship among members of the audience themselves than in one between the audience and a teacher behind the podium.

Notes

1. I must acknowledge my debt here to Peter Hawkes' unpublished "Guidelines for Preparing Collaborative Learning Worksheets."

Works Cited

Abel, Elizabeth, Marianne Hirsh and Elizabeth Langland, Eds. *The Voyage In: Fictions of Female Development*. Hanover, NH: University Press of New England, 1983.

Bruffee, Kenneth A. "The Brooklyn Plan: Attaining Intellectual Growth through Peer-Group Tutoring." *Liberal Education* 64, No. 4 (December 1978): 447-468.

Chodorow, Nancy. *The Reproduction of Mothering*. Berkeley, CA: University of California Press, 1978.

Dinesen, Isak. "The Blank Page." *Last Tales*. New York: Random House, Inc., 1957. 99-105.

Gilbert, Sandra M. and Susan Gubar. *Madwoman in the Attic: The Woman Writer and the Nineteenth-Century Literary Imagination*. New Haven, CT: Yale University Press, 1979.

Gilligan, Carol. *In a Different Voice: Psychological Theory and Woman's Development*. Cambridge, MA: Harvard University Press, 1982.

James, Henry. *The Bostonians*. New York: Modern Library, 1956.

Munich, Adrienne Auslander. "Feminist Criticism and the Literary Canon." Unpublished essay, 1984.

Showalter, Elaine. "Feminist Criticism in the Wilderness." *Critical Inquiry* 8 (1981): 179-206.

———. *A Literature of Their Own: British Women Novelists from Bronte to Lessing*. Princeton, NJ: Princeton University Press, 1977.

Transforming the Composition Classroom

Elisabeth Däumer and Sandra Runzo

It is helpful to remind ourselves how much our work as teachers resembles the work of our mothers. Both are women's work. Reimbursed little or not at all, such work hardly ever escapes, even when idealized, the connotations of "preparation" or "service" for a higher, presumably worthier entity or cause — whether it is "society," "the nation," or in the case of composition, the maintenance of standards of English studies and university education at large. Mothering and teaching partake in an important social function: the work of "socializing" and "civilizing." In raising children and teaching them to speak, the mother's task is to transmit the values and ideology of the society in which she lives. A "good" mother is expected to raise her children according to societal norms to assure that they become acceptable "citizens"; the teacher by instructing students in the proper use of the standard dialect, correct grammar, and the basic skills of literacy extends the maternal function into formal education (Ruddick, 342-367). Her work plays a similarly indispensable role as the mother's in the socialization and acculturation of the young to meet societal expectations and pressures.

Unlike mothering the teaching of writing is not, of course, exclusively women's work. Yet because of its low status it is more easily accessible to women; one recent commentator on the politics of composition implies that women belong to those applicants most welcome to composition teaching because they are, as he claims, "least likely to challenge devaluation" (Szilak, 27). If we look at the social attitudes toward women's work we find this shrewd observation solidly supported. Women's work is either not accorded the status of work in the sense of "labor"—a view that, in the case of housework and mothering, has been justified by referring to its "natural" or "instinctive" character; or, if admitted to be "labor," it is conceptualized in such ways that conspire to make questions of status and financial reimbursement contradictions in terms or indeed "unnatural."

This resemblance between the work of mothers and that of women teachers is traceable to the complex and far-reaching impact that the institution of motherhood has on *all* of women's work, including the teaching of writing. The ideal of motherhood as women's sacred calling has traditionally served to ridicule and to denigrate women, who, for a variety of reasons, pursued other work. Images of the schoolmarm, the prissy old maid, and exacting but relentlessly unimaginative "Miss Fidditch" come to mind, all of which picture the woman teacher as a "barren" woman, a spinster who in the estimation of society has failed at being a "real" woman—married and with children. In thus reducing women to a single function, their capacity to mother, institutionalized motherhood is equally responsible for the confinement and drudgery of most mothers' lives as it is for the reductive concepts that govern and constrain women's work and activities in general. The narrow definition of the composition classroom as a service course changed with the transmission of mechanical or purely technical skills, which still haunts the practice if not always the theory of writing instruction, is of particular pertinence here. It bears testimony to yet another attempt to oppressively constrain, limit, and control an activity that is inherently powerful and traditionally practiced by women—the teaching of language.

Despite the disheartening realities of our work as composition instructors, we need to keep in mind that we are involved in the teaching of language, and thus of the formation of thought and the creation of knowledge, even if these larger meanings are often unrecognizable in the term "composition" which designates, after all, the housework or dirty work of English departments. The problem we are facing then is how to unlock the possibilities inherent in our work, how to liberate its potential for personal growth and political transformation, and thereby foster the liberation of those students who have traditionally been denied equal participation in the creation of knowledge. Yet we believe that the problems of women are specific, and it is this specific place of women in culture and in the classroom that we have decided to focus on here. There are numerous models of "liberatory" teaching. The theories of Dale Spender, David Bleich, Richard Ohmann, and Paulo Freire have been taken into our account and have substantially contributed to the formulation of our ideas. We felt, however, an explicit need to also study the work of women composition theorists, in the hope that their thoughts about teaching, writing, and students, would answer the particular questions that arise from our experience as women and teachers. As our course assignments in the second part of the essay will show, we believe that the need for women to familiarize ourselves with the lives and thoughts of our foremothers is an imperative of feminist teaching. All the assignments address women's lives, writing, and thus specifically our women students. We think, however, that in the mixed sex classrooms most of us encounter as teachers, reading and writing assignments can easily be modified to include men.

We have two major strategies in mind that a feminist teacher might employ to transform the composition classroom into a feminist language classroom:

1) to draw on the life and practices of our first language teacher, the mother, for an understanding of the complexities of our role as teachers; and for the articulation of guiding values and ideals which stem from a radical critique of institutionalized mothering and the resultant vision of mothering as a primary locus for the transmission and the creation of women's language and culture;

2) to bring into the classroom the voices of women, those of our mothers or other women in our lives as well as those

that speak through literature, in order to explore wom-
en's relationship to language and to make students aware
of the rich and varied tradition of female articulation.

When we searched for women in the field of recent composition theory—as writers, teachers, theoreticians, and focus of
attention—we had not expected to discover what struck us as
a distinctly female perspective in the works of Janet Emig and
Ann Berthoff. Janet Emig is perhaps best known for her study
of the composing processes of 12th graders, which was ground-
breaking both in its methodology, the case study approach, and
its object, the writing process which at that time was still
deemed "unanalyzable." Emig's insistent challenging of preconceived notions about writing is also apparent in a short essay entitled "The Origins of Rhetoric: A Developmental View"
in which she calls for a reconceptualization of the role of the
teacher based on that of the mother's role in language development. Mothers, she observes, foster children's language acquisition by expanding their utterances: to a child's "Mommy
eggnog" the mother might respond with "Mommy had her eggnog." She is thus a collaborator in her child's first attempts at
articulation and a first nurturing and reassuring audience.
Transferring her insights to writing pedagogy, Emig suggests
that we can be most helpful to a writer when she is first formu-
lating her discourse by acting as collaborator and immediate
audience who expresses, in Emig's words, "with gentle tact
and concern the difficulties a trusted audience was having in
comprehending the discourse" (59). Because, as Emig's reference to language development suggests, writing is essentially a
natural activity, as teachers we should be devoted to creating
an environment that will enable students to write, one that is
safe and that inspires trust. The quality most essential for such
enabling teaching is our ability and willingness to let the ego
stand aside, a quality, Emig comments, she has rarely found in
men who tend to "teach as a revelation, as an expression of
ego" (132).

Though not inherently feminist, Emig's maternal perspective raises larger political implications. It challenges the value
of traditional classroom dynamics which in their adherence to

hierarchical structures and to external authority mirror patriarchal power relations. The maternal teacher no longer sees
herself as a judge who enforces external standards by grading
students' ability to comply with them. Rather, she attempts to
meet students on their own grounds, to individualize instruction, and to allow for self-sponsored writing by encouraging
students to interact as much with each other as with the instructor.

In insisting that composing is "the making of meaning,"
Ann Berthoff, like Emig, views the writer as a creative agent,
and the task of instruction as providing opportunities, or what
she calls "assisted invitations," to explore the composing process. Since, as she says, composing is the natural activity of the
inquiring mind, students learn to compose by becoming aware
of how their minds already compose, by "interpreting their interpretations" and "observing their observations." An assignment will ask them, for example, to daily record their observations of an organic, preferably unfamiliar object like crab legs, a
bird feather, or seaweed, and to observe themselves observing
these objects. In such assignments the maternal perspective
that we found so explicit in Emig's work, is also pervasive
though in a much less direct manner. There is a sense that
Berthoff wants to involve for her students their childhood
struggles and joys in grasping, with all their senses, the world
surrounding them, that she wants to remind them of a time
when the making of meaning held an enchanting new power.
Students, she claims, "learn to write by learning the uses of
chaos . . . [by] rediscovering the power of language to generate
the sources of meaning" (*The Making of Meaning*, 70).

What students learn in exploring their composing processes
is to tolerate ambiguity and to understand that meanings are
not fixed things but relationships. By observing their own perceptions and by naming them they create meanings which
they experience as dynamic, shifting, and constantly changing.
In becoming aware of the contextual nature of meaning, its dependence on the experience, perspective, and purpose of a
writer, Berthoff's students are prompted to cultivate capacities
that Carol Gilligan has found to characterize women's morality and thought: the appreciation of circumstance and context,

the tendency to say "it depends," the resistance to make absolute judgments.

A poignant and at times almost exuberant criticism of traditional writing instruction accompanies Emig's and Berthoff's
reliance on female identified values and practices. "Magical
Thinking" is Emig's term for the belief among many composition theorists that students only learn what we teach them. In
a similar vein, she announces the teaching of composition in
American high schools to be "essentially a neurotic activity"
(94), a judgment that is echoed in Berthoff's no less forceful re-
jection of what she views as a compulsive stress on hierarchical structures, categorizing, linear processes, outlining, and
persuasion and argumentation.

Both theorists' awareness of the transformative power of language and the need to have students discover and rediscover
this power for themselves shows deep affinities to the feminist
priorities of finding our voice and reclaiming our language and
culture. The work of both women offers us a place to start from
by acknowledging the social character of composing and its political implications, even if they do not themselves investigate
them, and by drawing on maternal practice and the values it
cultivates—such as creativity, cooperation, and responsive-
ness to individual needs and particular contexts—for their
vision of a language pedagogy that empowers and liberates
students.

Yet unless the politics of gender are explicitly included
among the social forces that inform the relationship between
learner and teacher, child and mother, we are unable to explain
how the very virtues of mothering, and women's work in general, have been exploited and subverted to stunt women's
growth and perpetuate their oppression. Emig's and Berthoff's
vision of maternal teaching idealizes mothering by taking into
account only one part of it, that part which enables and ex-
pands the child's language. Yet there is another side of maternal teaching that most of us also remember, where mothers silence their daughters in the name of society, where they mold
and bend their daughters' spirits and teach them to conform to
stifling definitions of femininity. It is only by studying the full
spectrum of mothers' lives that we can hope to understand the

apparent contradictions of maternal teaching and to conceive of it as a source of liberation. There are lessons to learn from the conflicting interests that make mothering an inescapably guilt-ridden experience for women: the pressure on a mother to make her daughter acceptable to a society that discriminates against women; her fear and guilt whether she complies with that pressure or resists it. If the cost of unacceptability is often ostracization, the cost of acceptability is not necessarily less severe for women: loss of self, loss of voice and creativity, deadening conformity. A mother's painful and confused question "What shall I teach my daughter?" which often, when it seems too late, haunts her life as a question after lost opportunities, after what she should or might have taught, is also the question that as feminist teachers we need to have asked ourselves. Any answer to this question will have to engage the mother-daughter relationship, its potential, in Rich's words, "for the deepest mutuality and the most painful estrangement" (*Of Woman Born,* 226).

In the feminist language classroom, the mother's arduous question of what to teach her daughter becomes the question of what language we want to teach our students, or rather, what we want to develop and foster in the classroom. Although many contemporary theorists and teachers state that writing, and by implication language, is a process of making meaning, for our women students, as well as for us, the making of meaning is a matter of the utmost importance. It is a matter of our very survival. Dale Spender says, in *Man Made Language,* that language is characterized by the silence of women and that women's silence empowers men while it perpetuates the myth of male superiority. The linguistic research of Julia Penelope (Stanley) and of others also documents women's invisibility in language. Many others, such as Adrienne Rich, Audre Lorde, and the French feminist theorists Hélène Cixous and Luce Irigaray claim that we have no words to express women's perspectives (such as on motherhood, on rape, on sexuality, and on our bodies) and that women's invisibility in history is the inevitable result of women's denigration in and exclusion from the structure and use of language. As these feminist language theorists have demanded, women need to rename ourselves and the world from our own and not from a male perspective. If we want to give our students the right to name themselves and their perceptions of reality, it is imperative that we reconsider the language we are assigned to teach in composition classes. How are we to reconcile the pervasive message in feminist theory that language oppresses women with the fact that it is exactly this language we are supposed to teach? While some of us will think that without the skills of "good" writing a student cannot truly be empowered, we must be equally aware that the qualities of "good" writing as they are advocated in textbooks and rhetoric books—directness, assertiveness and persuasiveness, precision and vigor—collide with what social conventions dictate proper femininity to be. Even should a woman succeed at becoming a "good" writer she will still have to contend with either being considered too masculine because she does not speak "like a Lady," or, paradoxically, too feminine and hysterical because she is, after all, a woman.[1] The belief that the qualities that make good writing are somehow "neutral" conceals the fact that their meaning and evaluation changes depending on whether the writer is a man or woman.

The same is true for the style of writing we are required to teach in most composition classes. While seemingly neutral it serves to convey an ideology that not only delimits how we can write but also about which we can write. Often, even when we diligently and conscientiously urge our students to write about issues of significance, we still primarily teach a style, whose distinctive features are detachment from others, suppression of emotion, a "logical"—i.e. hierarchical—organization, "appropriate" topic and word choice, persuasive strategies, and reliance on rules. This description of an accomplished writing style, found in virtually any rhetoric textbook, coincides, interestingly, with Carol Gilligan's description of what she calls the masculine mode of thought and morality. Gilligan infers from her observation of the differences in men's and women's characterization of relationships, particularly issues of dependency, that masculinity is defined through separation and femininity through attachment. Because the masculine mode of morality develops from the basic trait of separation, males learn to resolve ethical dilemmas by depersonalizing situations—by detaching themselves from others—and by trusting in an overriding structure of fair law and order. They enact a type of responsibility that is based on an assumption of aggression and adversarial relationships. The implication of Gilligan's observations is that most writing courses work toward the skillful incorporation of the masculine ethic, as Gilligan describes it, into students' writing. The language advocated by composition texts not only suppresses the feminine, but a student's achievement in a composition course will depend on how well she can further bury other, more feminist values in her language and in her writing. There is no guarantee, of course, that "out in the world" or even on her way through college this language will get her as far as a man.

If we want to enable our students to find a voice to combat the pervasive forces in our culture that silence women and others, who because of race, class, or other circumstances have been permitted less visibility and whose concerns have been suppressed, we must find ways of recovering women's voices and culture for our students. Yet, as Dale Spender has warned us, we ourselves are so much under the impression of male-governed notions about our language, that often we cannot "hear" what women's voices have to tell us. As with any other unexplored field, the way to learn about it is through careful and extensive study. But feminists from diverse disciplines have also realized from early on that their investigations of women's lives, history, psychology, or culture required them to develop new interpretive concepts that could account for the distinctness of women's experiences and perceptions. Our contention that women's voices, if only they were heard, can empower us, already implies an interpretive assumption that stems from our readings of women's writings and feminist theory: the conviction that there are areas in every woman's life where she actively constructs meaning, where she is not merely a victim but affirms values and ways of interacting and speaking with others that help her resist victimization. In the dialectic process of investigating and interpreting women's lives we render explicit the ways of acting and thinking that inform our lives either without our awareness or our ability to appreciate their significance. The inclusion of writings by women from various social and historical contexts—for example, slave women, working class women, pioneer women and immigrant women—indispensably assists in the classroom in our study of women's voices and grants validity to our project.

This process of rendering explicit what so far has been implicit has been performed by numerous feminists and, most recently, by Carol Gilligan and Sara Ruddick. Both maintain that because of their socialization and social practices women have developed distinct ethical values, concepts of thought, and ways of perceiving themselves, their relationships to others, and reality in general. Ruddick argues for the existence of "a conceptual scheme—a vocabulary and logic of contention" —which is rooted in women's social practice and through which those engaged in that practice understand and articulate their reality (318).

With the guidance of Gilligan and Ruddick our exploration of women's writings can reveal to us how women's perceptions of their everyday lives, of the particular circumstances of race and class, for example, have determined the language they use and the ways in which they take control of their lives or conceive of the possibilities of such control.

In addition to acknowledging that women, despite victimization, have been creators of their lives, the reading of women's works also serves the pedagogical purpose of establishing a language in class which students can use to talk about their own lives and perceptions. A consciousness of how social practice and language are intertwined will equip them to self-consciously reflect about the sources of their own language —its personal and social etymology—and the processes by which they formulate knowledge.[2]

The study of female slave narratives, for example, can illustrate the effect of social practice on writing as well as the complex language of written texts—that one text can consist of many languages. The writing by and about Black women not only depicts slavery but also confronts issues of work, education, family, anger, violence, and survival. However, as Erlene Stetson points out in her essay "Studying Slavery" (*But Some of Us Are Brave*, 61-84), slave women's narratives were often written by men and by white women but rarely by themselves;

but even authentic female slaves narratives reveal an almost total identification of the Black woman with white women. We, of course, cannot know how women's stories would have been different had their literacy been greater or had the coercion of the social structure not been so overwhelming. Yet the writing we have about Black women still tells us something about their lives and offers stunning examples of how women have been divested of their voices as well as examples of collaborating and conspiring in order to speak. Stetson notes that nineteenth-century writing about Black women by both Black and white women discloses the conflicts between the reality of Black women's lives and the social conventions that defined womanhood. White women's ambivalent descriptions of female slaves' lives, for example, implicitly challenge the moral structure of society: their writings grapple with the discord between their abhorrence of the enslavement of women and their belief in the virtue and desirability of the Cult of True Womanhood and the sanctity of the family for white as well as for Black women.[3]

Female slave narratives raise the issue of literacy as a crucial one for women. ("Two-thirds of the illiterate in the world today are women," Tillie Olsen reminded us in *Silences*, [184].) Class discussion could address the necessity of literacy—that women must have control of their language. Other discussions could revolve around untangling the contradictory attitudes within a piece of writing. Writing assignments stemming from such readings and discussions could focus on experiences of being unable, or denied the right, to speak for oneself and on incidents of racial, sexual, and linguistic oppression and assertion:

1) A student could discuss her identification with someone of a racial or social group different from her own.
2) Students could write about a time when someone changed or distorted their language. Such an assignment can also help students to weigh and distinguish between the need for women to speak for each other and the necessity that a woman speak for herself.
3) One student tells a story of personal significance to another who then retells it to the class. An ensuing discus-

sion could focus on the differences between written and spoken language and the complexities inherent in an oral tradition. The originator of the story could also describe how and whether her relationship to her words changed once another student conveyed them.

4) Students could write about each other—about their appearance, language use, etc.—and discuss the differences between how we perceive ourselves and how others perceive us.

5) A student could write about herself in a context that she thinks social conventions have generally denied her; for example, times whether remembered or imagined, where she felt powerful, aggressive, violent, angry, etc.

As some scholars have pointed out, to unearth the voices of women we must search out untraditional sources, often the forms of writing which have not been granted the status of literature because they are either personal (journals, letters, diaries) or community-based (Blues, spirituals, work songs). Paul Lauter notes, for example, that the literature of working class women, which is rooted in particular experiences and people, conveys a sense of the shared reality and shared values of working class people. Because they often did not have the literacy to produce the forms of art this culture regards as literary, they created oral forms of literature, "transitory" forms as Lauter calls them, which served immediate social and political purposes and spoke out of a communal context (*Women in Print I*, 109-134).

Michele Russell discusses how the Blues of Black women, the songs of Ma Rainey, Bessie Smith, and Billie Holiday, for instance, enables us to "*hear* the humanity" of Black lives and voices. The songs of these women give us their views on cultural institutions and political events and provide us as well with personal stories that depict the ways in which women have taken control over their bodies and lives and chronicle the hardship and the determination not to be defeated. In these songs women speak as social and political commentators, as members of a community, as independent spirits, as victims and survivors (Hull, Scott and Smith, *But Some of Us Are Brave*, 129-140).

In response to such stories students can consider their sense of self as members of a family of community and describe, and reflect upon, the stories passed on within that family or community. They could analyze, moreover, why they seem to choose some forms of expressing themselves and avoid others, and investigate how language either encourages or prevents the expression of rebellious feelings. As a class we could also examine how the ideology of womanhood affects our lives and possibility to choose. In Bessie Smith's song "Young Woman's Blues," for example, a young woman's sense of independence relies on her freedom to engage in sexual activity with whatever man she chooses. She describes herself as "lonesome" and abandoned by her lover, as anonymous and rootless, yet she revels in herself and seizes control of her body and her life.

The oral poem raises questions concerning the extent to which our ability to speak is bound to our control over our bodies and the correlation between sexuality and power. Writing assignments which would allow students to explore these issues are:

1) Write about a time when language helped you to cope with an emotionally difficult situation.
2) Consider the influence of institutionalized heterosexuality in our society. In what ways do you accept and reject societal pressures to date, to be part of a couple, to marry? And how does your own life—your family circumstances, sexual preference, experiences of violence, for example—affect the way you think and write about sexuality?
3) How do you see yourself? Write about your relationship to your body and any sense of power and vulnerability that results from your feelings about your body. This assignment could lead students to analyze the language they use to write about their bodies and to consider possible links between linguistic appearance and physical appearance.

Autobiographies, fiction, and speeches by women from diverse cultural backgrounds also document how women have named and renamed their experiences. Zora Neale Hurston's *Their Eyes Were Watching God* could focus a discussion of the different modes of women's expression and inspire students to explore the importance of talk in women's relationship—in Janie's friendship with Phoebe, in the meetings of the women in the community—as the means by which women pass on their culture and knowledge. The novel illustrates the power of naming oneself and of resisting other people's definitions. Janie challenges, and finally discards, her grandmother's insistence that for a Black woman the only aspiration in life should be to have a life like a white woman, to be put on a pedestal.[4] A classroom discussion of *Their Eyes* could be translated into writing assignments in which our students explore:

1) Their own identification with a woman's community.
2) The significance, or lack of significance, of female friendships in their lives.
3) Story telling as a means for passing on women's knowledge.
4) The power of definition and how definitions reveal one's self-interest and particular perspective. Definition papers on topics such as woman, work, talk, mother, family, sexuality, home, pleasure, dreams, etc., can demonstrate to students not only how ideas and values are individually defined, but also how social factors alter one's definitions.

In Tillie Olsen's "I Stand Here Ironing," a mother recollects the hardship of her working class life and the consequent suffering of her daughter Emily (*Tell Me a Riddle*, 73-89). A look at the mother's concerns and questions poignantly reveals how the daily drudgery of work, poverty, sickness, an unhappy marriage, and the demands of children thwart the mother's relationship with her daughter. Emily's teacher, wanting to understand Emily, turns to the mother, but the mother is stymied: How does she know what Emily needs? How can she help her daughter? The story raises crucial issues for our women students' relationships to their mothers, the power and powerlessness of mothers, a mother's anxieties about her own as well as her daughter's dreams, and the daughter's own anxieties. In responding to the mother-daughter relationship in the story, a student may consider the ways her mother's daily life affects their relationship and their understanding of each other. The possibility arises of engaging the discomforting issue of matrophobia—the fear of being like your mother—as well as the influence of a student's relationship with her mother on her attitude toward the woman teacher.

A specific assignment in which a student could explore her relationship with her mother and the affect of that relationship on language could be a "research paper" about her mother or about another woman who was particularly important to her while she was growing up. Students could pay particular attention to the place and meaning of language in their mother's lives and in their relationships to each other.

There are many other sources, of course, that feminist teachers can use in the classroom. We have suggested only a few that we have discovered while exploring the possibilities of bringing women's voices into the classroom. The simple truth that we continue to learn is that to hear women's voices we must read women's words. For our women students this is particularly important because women are acculturated into silence; not only are the lives and thoughts of women pushed to the periphery or beyond of recognized knowledge, but our students' own voices have been denied. We believe that the study of women's writing in the composition classroom will not only demonstrate for our women students the correlation of our actual lives with our language, but in enabling them to appreciate the power of women's knowledge and the strength women have cultivated through language, we can empower our students to seize control of their language, to make it truly their own.

Notes

1. See Robin Lakoff's *Language and Women's Place* (New York: Harper and Row, 1975), and Spender's *Man Made*

Language (London: Routledge and Kegan Paul, 1980), for a critique of Lakoff's work.

2. See for example, David Bleich's *Subjective Criticism* (Baltimore: The John Hopkins Press, 1978); Richard Ohmann's *English in America: A Radical View of the Profession* (New York: Oxford University Press, 1976). Pamela Annas bases her course "Writing as Women" on her recognition that women's daily lives affect their writing. A description of her course is available in *Women's Studies Quarterly* 12 (1984): 38-39, and a syllabus of her course is in the inaugural issue of *Feminist Teacher.*

3. While providing an excellent biography and invaluable references, Stetson also stresses the inaccessibility of many sources by and about black women and the urgent need for reporting.

4. See Lorraine Bethel's essay "'This Infinity of Conscious Pain': Zora Neale Hurston and the Black Female Literary Tradition," *But Some of Us Are Brave*, Eds. Gloria T. Hull, Patricia Bell Scott, and Barbara Smith (Old Westbury, NY: The Feminist Press, 1982), 176-188, for an interesting discussion of the centrality of storytelling and mythmaking in *Their Eyes.*

Works Cited

Annas, Pamela J. "Writing As Women" *Women Studies Quarterly* 12, No. 1 (Spring 1984): 38-39.

Berthoff, Ann E. *Forming Thinking Writing: The Composing Imagination.* Montclair, NJ: Boynton/Cook Publishers, Inc., 1982.

———. *The Making of Meaning: Metaphors, Models and Maxims for Writing Teachers.* Montclair, NJ: Boynton/Cook Publishers, Inc., 1981.

Emig, Janet. *The Web of Meaning: Essays on Writing, Teaching, Learning and Thinking.* Eds. Dixie Gosawi and Maureen Butler Montclair, NJ: Boynton/Cook Publishers, Inc., 1983.

Gilligan, Carol. *In a Different Voice: Psychological Theory and Women's Development.* Cambridge, MA: Harvard University Press, 1982.

Hurston, Zora Neale. *Their Eyes Were Watching God.* Urbana, IL: University of Illinois Press, 1978.

Lauter, Paul. "Working-Class Women's Literature: An Introduction to Study." *Women in Print I: Opportunities for Women's Studies Research in Language and Literature.* Eds. Joan E. Hartman and Ellen Messer-Davidow. New York: Modern Language Association, 1982. 109-143.

Lorde, Audre. "Poetry is Not a Luxury." *Sister Outsider.* Trumansburg, NY: The Crossing Press, 1984. 36-39.

———. "The Transformation of Silence into Language and Action." *Sinister Wisdom* 6 (1978): 11-15; rpt. *Sister Outsider.* Trumansburg, NY: The Crossing Press, 1984. 40-44.

Marks, Elaine and Isabelle de Courtivron. *New French Feminisms.* Amherst, MA: University of Massachusetts Press, 1980.

Olsen, Tillie. *Silences.* New York: Delacorte Press/Seymour Lawrence, 1978.

———. "I Stand Here Ironing." *Tell Me a Riddle.* Philadelphia: J. B. Lippincott, 1961. 73-89.

Rich, Adrienne. *Of Woman Born.* New York: W. W. Norton and Company, 1976.

———. *On Lies, Secrets, and Silence: Selected Prose 1966-1978.* New York: W. W. Norton and Company, 1979.

———. "The Transformation of Silence into Language and Action." *Sinister Wisdom* 6 (1978): 17-24.

Ruddick, Sara. "Maternal Thinking." *Feminist Studies,* 6, No. 2 (1980): 342-367.

Russell, Michele. "Slave Codes and Liner Notes." *But Some of Us Are Brave.* Eds. Gloria T. Hull, Patricia Bell Scott and Barbara Smith. Old Westbury, NY: The Feminist Press, 1982. 129-140.

Spender, Dale. *Man Made Language.* London: Routledge and Kegan Paul, 1980.

Stanley, Julia Penelope. "Prescribed Passivity: The Language of Sexism." *Views on Language.* Eds. Reza Ordoubadian and Walburga VonRaffler Engel. Murfreesboro, TN: Middle Tennessee State University, 1975. 96-108.

Stanley, Julia Penelope and Susan J. Wolfe. "Consciousness as Style, Style as Aesthetic." *Language, Gender and Society.* Eds. Barrie Thorne, Cheris Kramarae, and Nancy Henley. Rowley, MA: Newbury House Publishers, Inc., 1983. 125-139.

Stetson, Elaine. "Black Women in and out of Print." *Women in Print I: Opportunities for Women's Studies Research in Language and Literature.* Eds. Joan E. Hartman and Ellen Messer-Davidow. New York: Modern Language Association, 1982. 87-107.

———. "Studying Slavery: Some Literary and Pedagogical Considerations on the Black Female Slave." *But Some of Us Are Brave.* Eds. Gloria T. Hull, Patricia Bell Scott and Barbara Smith. Old Westbury, NY: The Feminist Press, 1982. 61-84.

Szilak, Dennis. "Teachers of Composition: A Re-Niggering." *College English* 39 (Sept 1977): 25-32.

Chapter Two

Awareness and Action:
The Teacher's Responsibility

This chapter focuses on teachers. This section comes before the chapter on students because it is the teacher's initial responsibility to develop awareness of the primacy of equity in the classroom and to act upon that awareness. It presents current research on student fear of writing and writing teachers and the teacher's own part in perpetuating this fear, and it sets forth a program for monitoring the teacher's linguistic behavior in the classroom.

The "Climate of Fear" in the Teaching of Writing

Alice S. Horning

Despite much recent research on writing from the perspective of both the teacher and the learner, too much of what goes on in the classroom is still based on a sense of fear that students have of both teachers and writing activity. The effect of the fear is to raise what second language acquisition researcher Stephen Krashen calls the Filter, which reduces the possibility of real learning taking place. The Filter is all of the learner's feelings, motivation, and sense of self as they play a role in the learner's ability to master the material under study. The goal of the writing teacher must therefore be to learn to understand the nature of the Filter, and to develop techniques for working with an awareness of it in such a way that students can learn to write effectively. An understanding of the Filter comes from a review of second language acquisition research on it; techniques for raising teachers' consciousness of the Filter derive from an analogy between teaching and the practice of medicine. From this context, moreover, we can begin to derive a series of ethnographic questions that merit further observation and analysis, and to suggest the directions such work should take.

The concept of the Filter was first developed in research on second language (L2) acquisition conducted by Heidi Dulay and Marina Burt, and was discussed in their article entitled "Remarks on Creativity in Language Acquisition." In this essay, Dulay and Burt describe the learner's central role in the teaching/learning process. They claim that the learner is engaged in a process of acquisition in the mastery of L2, and that in the process, the learner constructs, internally and unconsciously, the system of rules and principles by which a language is governed. The process is controlled to some degree by what Dulay and Burt first called "affective delimiters":

Affective delimiters refer to conscious or unconscious motives or needs of the learner which contribute, among other things, to : 1) individual preferences for certain input models over others, 2) prioritizing aspects of language to be learned, and 3) determining when language acquisition effects should cease. For example, depending on various criteria, a learner will "tune-in" more to certain speakers of the language rather than to others, or learners will learn certain types of verbal routines or vocabulary items rather than others, or learners will apparently stop acquiring the target language at a point before they reach native-like proficiency. These behaviors may be attributed to affective factors which delimit to a significant extent the input data which is made accessible to the cognitive organizers (99).

With regard to L2 acquisition, then, Dulay and Burt claim that affective factors limited how much of the new language learners could take in and make use of in the process of mastering the L2. A learner with an open, confident attitude toward L2 was thought more likely to succeed in mastery of it.

In the past five years, the concept has undergone much revision, and additional research has changed and sharpened it. In *Language Two*, Dulay, Burt and Stephen Krashen describe the Filter this way:

The filter is that part of the internal processing system that subconsciously screens incoming language based on what psychologists call "affect": the learner's motives, needs, attitudes, and emotional states. The filter appears to be the first main hurdle that incoming language data must encounter before it is processed further (46).

Clearly, since the Filter is the "first main hurdle" that language must pass before the learner can begin to acquire it, it plays a critical role in the learning process. Indeed, Dulay, Burt and Krashen point out that:

Research evidence indicates that the successful acquisition of com-
municative skills in the new language depends *primarily* on filter-
ing . . . (72, emphasis mine)

Teachers of writing may wonder about the relevance of L2 acquisition research to the teaching and learning of writing. I
have argued elsewhere that there is an important relationship
between second language learning and learning to write, at
least for basic writers, and very possibly for all writers (Horning, *Teaching Writing*). Other researchers have made a stronger
case by pursuing various lines of research,[1] and there is only
limited evidence that contradicts the application of L2 theory
to the development of writing skills (Neilson). Although the
two processes are not exactly alike, the similarity is clearly
strong enough to allow the application of the concept of the
Filter from L2 research to writing.

There are four key elements in the Filter, all of which may be
important for writing students: personality factors, anxiety
levels, peer identification and motivation to learn the language
(Dulay, Burt and Krashen, 4). The personality factors that have
been examined have to do with how the learner views the
teacher and other speakers of the second language. Dulay, Burt
and Krashen note that: ". . . language learners, consciously or
unconsciously, select only certain types of people as models
worth emulating" (4). Similarly, especially for basic writers,
how the teacher and others in the academic environment present themselves may be a key factor. Basic writers may only
succeed when the instructor gives them a real sense that they
can and will do so, and makes this possibility an attractive one.
Bear in mind that this process may be unconscious, and thus, is
not always something that can be observed directly. Ethnographic research might allow us to observe this interaction in a
useful way. Among the questions for research in this context
are these: How are aspects of personality and modeling behaviors communicated in classroom and conference interactions?
What does a teacher of writing do in conference that s/he
doesn't do in the classroom?

Anxiety level, the second factor in the Filter, can certainly be high in a second language class. Readers of this paper can undoubtedly recall a time in high school or college French or Spanish when they slumped down behind their textbooks hoping that the teacher would not call on them for fear of having to pronounce the new language. Worse was having to read aloud from the book or act out a spontaneous dialogue in front of the class. Dulay, Burt and Krashen report more than a half-dozen studies showing a relationship between low anxiety and successful language acquisition (52-53), as well as other research on successful relaxation techniques which enhance classroom performance (51-52).

Anxiety levels can be raised or lowered in a writing class. They can be raised by the ways in which instructors respond to student writing (consider the effect of the paper that is returned awash in red ink), and by the way instructors respond to students' other work. In practice on grammar and mechanics, students often sit for many moments over a practice sentence, fearing that wherever they put the comma, apostrophe, or whatever, will be wrong. Years of such experience batter the ego and raise the anxiety level of the learner. But other kinds of classroom behavior can lower anxiety. Students can be encouraged to develop and to demonstrate their expertise in certain areas or aspects of writing, both mechanical and rhetorical. Betty Rizzo's *The Writer's Studio* for instance, encourages group work, and encourages students to teach one another. Even weak students are remarkably good teachers if they have had an opportunity to master the lesson beforehand. For many of us, real learning does not take place until we have to teach what we have learned to someone else. It is easy to designate a fairly proficient thesis writer or first paragraph writer as class expert and let others consult with him/her. A sense of mastery and expertise, even if only in one area, lowers anxiety and can enhance learning in all areas. The student teachers convey their sense of self-confidence, a phenomenon which warrants ethnographic study.

These kinds of actions reshape the whole feeling of the classroom in teaching writing. Ethnographic study makes it possible to examine the ways in which the teacher becomes less the final arbiter of right and wrong, and more just one, but not the only, member of the audience for whom the student is writing for. Simultaneously, the students' sense of themselves as writers and readers, capable of making their own judgments and having opinions just as valid as the teacher's, is enhanced. The new balance is hard to achieve if the teacher feels that maintaining power and control is important, but worth the effort. Behaving in this manner, the teacher acknowledges the importance of the Filter as a phenomenon that can enhance or impede learning. A careful analysis of the teacher's behavior in response to ethnographic questions can shed light on such issues as why some teachers succeed in certain types of classes rather than others (lectures or seminar, for instance), and what makes a good writing teacher able to free students to express themselves on paper.

This attitude of sharing the work in learning to write addresses and fosters peer identification, the third element in the Filter. Peer identification has to do with how much the learner identifies with the group that speaks the second language. Dulay, Burt and Krashen define this aspect of the Filter as follows:

The language or language variety one speaks is often a signal to others that one belongs to a certain social group. The *social group identification motive* may thus be defined as the desire to acquire proficiency in a language or language variety spoken by a social group with which the learner identifies (50).

The extent to which a writing student identifies with academically successful members of the peer group in the class or school will have some effect on the Filter. In a basic writing class, setting each student up as an expert in some area of study, like writing an opening paragraph or thesis sentence, as described above, tends to work very well, because then each student can identify with and try to emulate the success of others. Ultimately, if the identification is strong enough, every student comes to succeed in every aspect of the writing process. The ethnographic questions here are: By what process does this identification occur and how can it be enhanced? What do teachers say and do to make the identification process work?

The last and in some ways most complex element in the Filter is motivation. The classic study on motivation in L2 acquisition was done by Gardner and Lambert in 1959. In the study, Gardner and Lambert made a distinction between integrative and instrumental motivation: integrative motivation is usually motivation to learn a language in order to become a member of the community where the language is spoken, while instrumental motivation is a drive to learn for utilitarian reasons such as to do well academically, to get a job, to pass a course, and so on (*Language Two*, 48). Both types of motivation enhance language writing.

Are writing students well motivated to learn to write? Sometimes, but not always. Often the motivation is strictly instrumental, and while that helps, students are more likely to succeed if they are integratively motivated as well. Teachers must be aware of the fact that in the absence of motivation or in the presence of actual hostility (as a result of being placed in a remedial writing class, for example), the Filter is likely to be a restrictive one.

So far, we've looked at the Filter for L2 acquisition as a powerful device that controls the amount of learning the student does. The Filter involves the learner's personality, anxiety level, peer identification and motivation. The effective teaching methods I have described are not new, and good teachers have been following them for years. However, many teachers *don't* use them, and to help those who are not converted, we need to understand more clearly how such methods work and how they can be enacted. If teachers adopt a new idea, but don't really believe in it or don't fully integrate it into their overall behavior, they may very well send signals that contradict or even sabotage the new method. They will wonder then why it didn't succeed. We therefore need to ask ethnographic questions about *successful* methods, questions that must be answered if we are to understand not just what a good teaching practice "is," but to see how it penetrates all aspects of teacher behavior. As ethnographers have been arguing for some time, we need to study ethnographically not just the failures, but the successes in education. To help pose the questions clearly, since teachers may tend to see their classrooms from their own points of view, they can be reminded of a context in which they more nearly occupy the same position their students do—namely, dealing with a doctor and particularly a pediatrician, who may easily make one feel "graded" in one's performance as a parent.

Unlike most situations in medicine where the central relationship is between the doctor and the patient, pediatrics uniquely involves a parent as a deeply involved third party. The teaching function of doctors emerges most clearly in pediatrics because parents, especially new parents, are so uninformed and need so much information. If this information is delivered in a "climate of fear" like the one in the writing classroom, a feeling of failure and stupidity results for parents. Good pediatricians are good teachers who, with an awareness of the Filter, can encourage parents to learn and trust their own judgment about their children. The whole relationship of parent and pediatrician can serve as a useful model for the teaching of writing, as I have argued elsewhere ("Medical Model," 51-58).

Using the medical situation as an analogy, we can review the elements of the Filter, beginning with the first which has to do with personality. The learner must view the teacher either consciously or unconsciously as a person to be emulated. The parent in the medical situation must see the doctor as a knowledgeable person worth emulating in terms of his or her ability to diagnose and treat a child's health problem. Parents cannot learn to do their own diagnoses, but they must learn to work cooperatively with doctors and adopt their general confidence in handling children. Doctors convey this sense largely by their behavior when they see patients and parents in their offices. Our pediatrician, for example, spends a lot of time with us, asking both specific questions about the child's illness and general behavior, and also asking questions which address my judgment about the situation. The discussion often builds my confidence about my ability to learn how to take care of my children and keep them healthy. In addition, our doctor seems to make an extra effort to be accessible for me to check my judgment when my child is sick or well. This accessibility on her part helps me as a learner when I am feeling uncertain about a judgment I've made.

These points carry over directly to the teaching of writing. My pediatrician, using her awareness of the Filter and its importance to learning, has enabled me to learn to handle my children as a function of the interaction of her "teaching style" and my personality. Writing teachers can do many of the same things to enhance the learning of writing students. Teachers need to be able to diagnose students' writing problems and to do so with confidence. As one of my students said on a course evaluation, the sense that, whatever writing problem one has, it can be treated and resolved, is a view that fosters confidence in students. The same attitude can help students work cooperatively with their teachers to solve their writing problems jointly.

But teachers have to be willing to spend the time sitting down, seeing each student individually and frequently, explaining and answering questions until the student is satisfied and can do the work that has been assigned. In asking and answering questions, teachers can convey the same kind of general concern about students that our pediatrician conveys about patients. Sometimes, important and relevant information about the student as a writer can turn up, and sometimes, just conveying the sense of caring is a sufficient acknowledgment of the Filter to allow success in learning. In fact, there is research which shows that having students in for conferences can have a positive effect on their overall success rate in college.[2]

Of course, accessibility is not just a matter of announced office hours, but rather, an attitude, which is perceived by students. In an ethnographic context, several questions evolve: What specific behavior *communicates* the teacher's attitude or approach to success or failure rates, particularly where anxiety is concerned? And what specific student behaviors relate to these situations? How could one dispassionately *observe* the close, often intimate student relationship in the conference or classroom contexts that reveal this information? A colleague of mine has been looking into this problem with an informal experiment. She has been tape recording her student writing conferences with a hand-held dictaphone recorder. The machine is small enough so that, after a few minutes, the student more or less ignores its presence. Yet, it provides a way of being able to recreate and analyze the interaction and messages between student and teacher. These tapes might yield much useful information to answer the questions raised above.

When students work on their writing individually, they often need to come in and reconfirm their judgment, and in the process have their confidence level raised. Every time I see students in the office in this context, I am acknowledging the presence of the Filter and making it more possible for students to learn to write well. When students learn to emulate me as a person who can understand and solve writing problems, they are quite far along toward themselves being able to understand and to solve their own writing problems; they are on their way from being apprentice writers to being mature writers, capable of working alone and of solving their own problems with a writing task.

A teacher's accessibility at just the right moment can play a key role in the development of writing skills. During my first year in college, for instance, I had a wonderful instructor for the standard (at the time) composition and literature course offered to beginning students. The assignment was the last of the term, and I remember choosing to write about Brecht's *Mother Courage.* I needed help with the opening paragraph. The rest of it had gone fairly well, and I was deeply involved in the writing. But I couldn't figure out how to start, as openings have always been a problem for me. Fortunately, the day I chose to stop by, my instructor was in his office and available to give me a hand. I actually wrote the opening paragraph on the spot, with him watching and guiding me. He was able to both supervise my writing of this particular opening and to assist me in mapping a general strategy for starting papers. This session helped me work independently a number of times thereafter in writing an introduction or in judging one I had written. Certainly these interactions, too, point towards ethnographic investigation.

The second element of the Filter is the learner's anxiety level. Any parent who has coped with a seriously ill child, even temporarily, knows the anxiety that is often present during a visit to the doctor's office. Anxiety at the pediatrician's can often be present even when illness is not, or at least is not apparent. There is always the nagging sense, even when a child seems fine, that some problem will turn up. The higher the anxiety level, the harder it is to learn. Anxiety can also be high when the doctor finds a problem that the parent did not even know existed.

The fear of error is a major cause of anxiety for writing students, many of whom still believe that good writing is equivalent to correct writing. And even those who don't would like to believe that there is a formula for everything and a sure, correct way to handle every part of the writing process. There are at least two ways to lower student anxiety about error in writing. One of these is to understand errors from an analytical perspective, as advocated by Shaughnessy and as approached by L2 researchers (*Language Two*, 138-199), and make use of the research that has been done on error patterns in L2 research as advocated by John Schafer. A second is to give students the freedom to err without guilt and anxiety, and especially, without penalty of grades. The approach that is most effective in this case is the use of revision. In my approach to regular first year student composition, students do at least two drafts of three or four of their papers, and I have recently considered the notion of having them do one paper that they work on in multiple drafts over the whole term. Such an exercise would give students the experience of working in the same manner as mature, proficient writers, who hardly ever feel really "done" with a piece of writing. It is possible, then, to lower anxiety by understanding error and giving students the freedom to commit errors as they are engaged in the writing process. Teachers must, if they wish to convey this sense that errors are okay, understand how what they say and how they say it influences students' sense of freedom. This understanding may come from ethnographic studies of student-teacher interaction.

The third element in the Filter is peer identification, the desire to be part of the group that speaks the L2. The central issue here is not one of social climbing so much as it is one of equality. The L2 learner simply wants to be equal to and be accepted by speakers of the target language. Among writing students, and particularly among basic writers, the drive is to develop writing skills on a par with those of other students. When I tell students the goal of a writing course is to give them skills good enough so that what they write will be judged on substantive merit and not on how it is written, they seem to understand this goal and accept it as a reasonable outcome of learning to write.

One superb equalizing strategy lies in the use of sentence combining. One of my great surprises in starting to use sentence combining in teaching composition was the students' response and their sense that they were all equal in confronting a combining exercise. Sentence combining also works well in helping students emulate one another, so that those who are capable of greater stylistic sophistication serve as models for those who need to develop their style more fully. Moreover, sentence combining helps show students that there are no necessarily right answers in writing. Sentence combining activity, whether drawn from a book or even more effectively drawn from students' own writing, can foster peer identification.

In a similar way, we can make students realize that while some people are better writers than others, no one is really an expert, and everyone can use the same tactics when approaching a writing task. This message seems to underlie much of Linda Flower's approach to the teaching of writing in *Problem-Solving Strategies for Writing.* She advocates that student writers make use of the same strategies used by successful writers as documented in her research and that of others using writing protocols. When teachers tell students about their own writing problems, they create this same sense of equality.

A similar kind of equality may pervade a writing workshop where personal computers with word processing are used for writing, and where students share terminals and look over one another's shoulders to watch the writing process go on. Classes using word processing at Oakland University function this way, and at least one instructor has reported a marked benefit from having students share their work with one another in a

writing community created by the close quarters around the
terminals (Sudol interview). Because the use of computerized
word processing is still in its infancy, it may be too soon to
judge its impact on writing. But as the use of computers in
writing classes increase, ethnographers will be able to address
the question of writing communities that are formed in this
way. The interaction among students looking at a text on a
screen is clearly different than that of the same students looking at a typed page, and it will be most interesting to see how
the motivation anxiety factors are affected by this context.

Another sense in which equality is derived comes from the
last element in Filter, motivation. The sense which must be
conveyed if motivation is to be enhanced is the sense that
teacher and student work together as a team to develop the
student's writing skills. Where does the sense of a team effort
come from? Looking at the medical situation, except when a
patient is under complete supervision in a hospital, every medical problem requires the joint effort of the physician and the
patient. Doctors can prescribe all they want to, but if the patient fails to follow the prescription faithfully, no cure or resolution of the problem will occur. In pediatrics, joint effort is
equally important, or perhaps more so because children are
generally unable, really, to help themselves. Parents usually
have both instrumental and integrative motivation to help
their children get well. But this motivation is easily squashed
by a doctor with the wrong attitude, who does not believe in
getting parents to work jointly on a problem.

The "joint effort" attitude is implied strongly by the doc-
trine of "informed consent": the requirement that a physician
disclose material facts and present alternatives to a patient
before treatment and then obtain consent (Abram, 94), particularly for experimental procedures. Our pediatrician follows
these requirements in treating my children by explaining what
she thinks the problem is, why she thinks what she does, and
what she wants us to do about it. Such dialogue (and it is a *dialogue*) plays a crucial role in health care:

. . . studies confirmed by intuition that dialogue has therapeutic value.
The studies showed that well-informed patients do indeed get better

faster, are frequently less anxious and—contrary to medical myth —are less likely to refuse treatment than poorly informed patients (94).

In conducting this dialogue with me and requiring me to make informed choices, our pediatrician teaches me something about illness and suggests by implication that between us we can solve the problem. In teaching writing, it is important to give similar explanations of what a student's writing problems are how to go about solving them. It is an approach which takes time, but also an approach which makes it more likely that students will "get better"—as writers—faster. Moreover, it is an approach which warrants detailed ethnographic study.

All four elements of the Filter pose a series of questions, noteworthy in their call for ethnographic investigation:

-What is there in teacher behavior which creates or lowers anxiety for students, and how is that communicated?

-What school-induced forms of anxiety carry over to the writing classroom, or is the writing class unique in the anxiety it creates? What in the students' individual histories contributes?

-How is the classroom community a cultural perpetrator of attitudes towards writing? Is the teacher able to modify any attitude which seem to affect students adversely? Why? How? What might s/he do?

-What in the classroom context seems especially motivational in terms of "lowering the Filter?" Why?

What else does or could the teacher do? Are there steps the teacher might take to change the motivational factors outside the classroom, and, if so, what are they?

All these are important questions which could initiate an ethnographic, observational study of fear and writing. *Why*, simply, do some things "work" only in specific contexts like conferences, and not in others, like classrooms?

If writing teachers proceed with a strong awareness of the Filter, the chances for learning increase because more new information can get inside the student where it can be absorbed and used. Writing is, for so many students, such a loaded and fearful activity, and writing teachers so awesome and scary with their red pens forever poised for a pounce, that students must always have some fear upon crossing the threshold of the writing classroom. The concept of the Filter helps to break down student writers' fears into manageable elements of personality, anxiety, peer identification or equality, and motivation. The analogy of teaching writing to the quasi-teaching situation that exists in a pediatrician's office illustrates ways of informing teaching with an awareness of the Filter so that students learn and master writing skills. Knowing that the Filter is there, and using the approaches described here can help writing teachers reach those goals. Ethnographic evaluation, observing the behaviors and interactions of students and teachers in a community context, can perhaps help us apply these approaches given the dynamic, often changing needs of our classroom situations as we recognize and analyze behaviors that positively and negatively affect our students' abilities to learn.

Notes

1. See, for instance, Robert L. Allen, "Written English Is a 'Second Language', "*Teaching High School Composition*, Eds. Gary Tate and Edward P. J. Corbett (New York: Oxford University Press, 1970), 348-357; or Barry M. Kroll and John C. Schafer, "Error-Analysis and the Teaching of Composition," *College Composition and Communication* 29 (October 1978): 242-248.

2. See, for example, Ernest Pascerella and Patrick Terenzini, "Patterns of Student-Faculty Informal Interaction Beyond the Classroom and Voluntary Freshman Attrition," *Journal of Higher Education* 48 (1977): 540-552; also discussed by Alexander W. Aston in *Preventing Students from Dropping Out* (San Francisco: Jossey-Bass, 1975); and in *Four Critical Years: The Effects of College on Beliefs, Attitudes and Knowledge* (San Francisco: Jossey-Bass, 1977).

Works Cited

Abram, Morris. "Ethics and the New Medicine." *New York Times Magazine.* 5 June 1983. 94.

Dulay, Heidi and Marina Burt. "Remarks on Creativity in Language Acquisition," *Viewpoints on English as a Second Language.* Eds. Marina Burt, Heidi Dulay and Mary Finocchiaro. New York: Regents Publishing Company, Inc., 1977. 95-126.

Dulay, Heidi, Marina Burt and Stephen D. Krashen. *Language Two.* New York: Oxford University Press, 1982.

Flower, Linda. *Problem-Solving Strategies for Writing.* New York: Harcourt, Brace, Jovanovich, Inc., 1981.

Gardner, Robert C. and Wallace E. Lambert. "Motivational Variables in Second-Language Acquisition." *Canadian Journal of Psychology* 13, No. 4 (December 1959): 266-272.

Horning, Alice S. "A Medical Model for Teaching Basic Writing." *English Quarterly* 14, No. 2 (Summer 1981): 51-58.

————. *Teaching Writing as a Second Language: An Inquiry.* Typescript, 1981.

Kroll, Barry M. and John C. Schafer. "Error-Analysis and the Teaching of Composition. *College Composition and Communication* 29 (October 1978): 242-248.

Neilson, Brooke. "Writing as a Second Language: Psycholinguistic Processes in Composition." Diss. University of California at San Diego, 1979.

Rizzo, Betty. *The Writer's Studio: Exercises for Grammar, Proofreading, and Composition,* 2nd ed. New York: Harper and Row Publishers, Inc., 1982.

Shaughnessy, Mina P. *Errors and Expectations: A Guide for the Teacher of Basic Writing.* New York: Oxford University Press, 1977.

Sudol, Ronald A., Associate Professor of Rhetoric. Oakland University, Personal Communication, June 23, 1983.

Hearing Is Believing: The Effect of Sexist Language on Language Skills[1]

Alice F. Freed

Language and equity; communication and fairness; speaking, writing and power. A short excursion into these areas convinces even the most casual observer that s/he has entered the domain of the interaction between language in the abstract and the reality of life in our society—the intricate and fascinating connection between language and culture and between language and thought. We must look beyond the well-known details of language structure and language as skills and into the vast array of social implications carried by language. The study of these subjects is far from simple, and, as we will explore below, the teaching of these topics presents some very special difficulties.

One of the great problems in teaching anything about language is making students aware of their own speech and of the world of words around them. It is indeed a challenge to create for people what we may call a conscious awareness of language since, every waking hour of our lives, we speak and respond to our language automatically, usually without thinking about it at all. Whether struggling with foreign language instruction, analysis of literature, writing skills and composition, or introductory courses in linguistics or other related topics, teachers face similar problems. How do you direct students to see and hear what actually takes place in language and then have them focus appropriate attention on those particular aspects of language which deserve special and careful scrutiny?

Here our concern is not only that of making students cognizant of the structure of sentences, the possible grace of various phrases, the cohesiveness of paragraphs and texts, and the stylistic nuances that can be conveyed by different words or constructions. We wish, in addition, to show them how words, sentences and written ideas in general communicate, perpetuate, and even create attitudes about social issues, in particular attitudes of unfairness or prejudice towards women (or men).

In a book about composition and language equity, the first issue is specifically how to create awareness on the part of the students of the ways in which language can convey inequity. In order to correct inequity in writing (or speaking), people must first be able to identify such features in what they read or in what they hear. It is not unlike the foreign language instructor who must first teach students to hear the distinction between two sounds in a new language before expecting them to produce the phonetic differences in question. In order to write with an eye to fairness, students must first be sensitized to the lack of fairness in the language they read and in the language that they hear around them.

It is my belief that the gender-related language forms that we are exposed to and that we acquire as we learn our first language contribute significantly to the ways in which we view one another as men and women and frame for us our respective expectations. Since writing usually reflects the world view of the person composing, sexist language will inevitably show up in the work of our students unless we familiarize them with the issues of language and gender. This is crucial for successful teaching of composition from a feminist perspective. For the purposes at hand, we will pay particular attention to the language to which students are exposed in classroom lectures and in texts. Unfortunately, quite aside from what they may experience in their personal lives, students continue to be confronted with sexism in college classrooms—and most often this type of linguistic injustice, occurring so close to the heart of learning, goes unnoticed and worse, unchallenged. While many professional organizations, various publishers and a variety of scholars have published suggestions on how to handle ambiguous, inaccurate, stereotypic, or discriminating reference to women and men in scholarly writing, few have addressed themselves to the questions raised in this book: sexist language and the teaching of composition. Equally striking is the fact that sexist language in the classroom, that is, the language used by teachers and professors when addressing captive groups of students, has also been largely neglected. It is this type of sexist language and what it conveys to our students that will be the focus of what follows.[2]

Below, I will make several suggestions of things that writing instructors can do (1) to monitor their own speech in the classroom, (2) to sensitize their students to the linguistic issues at hand and (3) to get students to incorporate these observations into their written work. The emphasis will be on spoken not written language because the thesis here is that sensitivity to language for composition must be preceded by awareness of language inequity in what is heard, in what is said, and in what is read. The first step, obvious as it may seem, is to explain fully and clearly the existence and the content of sexist language and at the same time to refrain from alienating those who are threatened by any suggestion of language change. People writing about sexism in language usually write with a certain amount of passion. The issues are vital, the stakes are high and resistance to linguistic change is enormous. We need to demonstrate clearly that such change is a natural and important part of the life of a language.

We may say that prejudicial language in general is language, in the form of specific words or phrases, which comments on the nature of an individual (or group) by generalizing or stereotyping about a larger group to which that person or persons belong. The group may be identified by biological similarities (sex, race, height, etc.) or by social organization (religion, nationality, political beliefs, etc.). More particularly, sexist language is any language form which isolates or stereotypes some aspect of an individual's nature (or the nature of a group of individuals) based on their sex. This results from preconceived notions about women and men. Other definitions, taken from Mary Vetterling-Braggin's collection of essays on sexist language, are as follows: "A word or sentence is sexist if and only if its use creates, constitutes, promotes or exploits an unfair or irrelevant distinction between the sexes" (Vetterling-Braggin,

3). "A word or sentence is sexist if and only if its use contributes to, promotes, causes, or results in the oppression of either
sex" (4).

There is a great similarity in these definitions, and the slight
differences among them are not of importance to us. However,
there are other definitions which include more than we intend
here. For example, in their 1972 article "One Small Step for
Genkind," Miller and Swift state that "sexist language is any
language . . . that assumes the inherent superiority of one sex
over the other" (99). We must distinguish between these two
types of definitions.

What is needed is a clear differentiation between "sexist language" and "sexist thoughts or ideas." In all cases where it is
specifically the language form that is objectionable, there is
some other work (or words) that can be substituted for the
sexist form or specific words can be changed or deleted to re-
move the sexism. Here we are dealing explicitly with "sexist
language." Of course, sexist attitudes underlie all such cases of
sexist language even if one wishes to argue that many cases of
linguistic sexism have simply become a matter of convention
and habit. Since sexist language teaches and encourages sexist
beliefs, these mechanical manifestations of sexism cannot be
dismissed as unimportant. In addition, there is the verbal expression of sexist thought; this results in sexist statements
which are a reflection of the sexist ideas of the speaker. The
only alteration that can be made to such statements is to eliminate them directly, which means to somehow eliminate the
ideas that create them. In such cases, it is not the language *per
se* that is sexist but rather the underlying attitudes or ideas of
the speaker.

It is with great difficulty that I can object to the language of
such a statement as "Women are lousy drivers." The statement is obviously sexist, discriminatory and one which negatively stereotypes women by grouping all individuals sharing
only one characteristic—their biological gender—into one
category. But if an individual possesses such an attitude and
cannot be convinced to change it, there is nothing that I can
suggest to correct the expression of that belief. If, on the other

hand, someone says or writes, "Young men and young girls are all lousy drivers," there is something specifically linguistic which can be pointed out. The phrase can be corrected with a parallel construction as in "young men and young women are all lousy drivers." It is clear that we must work to eliminate both types of statements, understanding that the basis for them is identical, but we must also recognize that the specific problems to be addressed are not the same and may require different strategies of attack. Unfortunately, both types of sexist comments are frequently found in and out of the classroom, in writing and in speaking. My preliminary goal is to correct the specifically linguistic bias with the hope that the awareness that will be generated by these changes will lead to changes in other areas of verbal and written expression as well.

A first important step in sensitizing students to the language around them is to have them keep journals which are intended to be collections of sexist comments which they hear around them. The focus should be on sexist language forms that they hear or read in academic settings (in classroom, students' meetings, discussion groups, etc.) and in readings which have been assigned through any of their classes. Students may be asked to record verbal exchanges or specific language forms that make them feel diminished or just uncomfortable, perhaps even uncomfortable for someone else. As a second step, writing assignments may be made which ask students to describe one of the experiences which they recorded. This can be a narrative or fictional account of the social, emotional or academic impact of the experience.

Of particular interest is the language which they encounter in the college classroom; it is a sad fact that we can be almost guaranteed that our students will come up with numerous examples. The possibilities for expression of sexist attitudes is nearly limitless in a classroom setting. Personal evaluative comments and interpretations by a professor are commonplace and are actually expected in the discussion of sociological, psychological, biological, economic, anthropological, historical or literary issues, to name just a few. The academic freedom which we so carefully guard and which permits and encourages individual selection of texts, examples and presentation of material also allows for a protected environment for the perpetuation of prejudicial stereotypes.

We may make a number of specific recommendations which should be helpful to professors wishing to monitor their own speech as well as to those who want to communicate to their students techniques of correction for speaking and writing. Again, it is important to repeat that the elimination of unfair language in writing follows most successfully from an awareness of such language in what one hears and reads. Some of the suggestions are of special interest to speakers while others are similar to the ones made for eliminating sexism in writing. All of them deserve to be mentioned here, however, since we wish to emphasize the fact that these features of language are as important to monitor in informal speech as in informal writing. Perhaps it is more difficult to avoid sexism in speaking, in part because we do not have a chance to go back over what we have said in order to evaluate whether or not we have been evenhanded in our choice of words. So it does require re-education and it certainly takes a willingness to consciously choose one word over another. This sort of careful selection of words and phrases is precisely what we want to communicate to our students.

The following are some suggestions:

1. When speaking to a class (or group) of men and women (or girls and boys), deliberately alternate between *he* and *she* for indefinite pronominal reference. Another alternative is to say *he or she* as in the sentence "When a linguist is analyzing data, he or she should consider all available interpretations of the material."
2. When speaking of a hypothetical student, subject, informant, patient, client, writer, researcher or other randomly chosen human, do not assume the sex of the individual.
3. Avoid the generic use of *man*; instead use *humans*.
4. Avoid stereotyped and fixed phrases which express bias such as *man and wife, fathers and sons, forefathers,* etc.
5. When speaking, do not assume the sex of individuals

based on their occupation. That is, do not assume when speaking that all doctors are men, that all nurses are women, that all bosses are men, that all secretaries are women or that all parents are mothers. They are not.

6. Use parallel constructions and word choices when referring to women and men. Avoid phrases such as *men and girls, men and ladies,* or *Dr. Kissinger and Nancy,* etc.

7. Purposely choose non-conventional, non-traditional examples of your own when speaking, in order to break expected stereotypes. For example, speak of a boss who asks her secretary if he can work overtime.

8. Avoid making jokes which are at the expense of any portion of your audience—however innocent you may think the comments are. One way of doing this is be eliminating so-called "wife-jokes," etc. and by eliminating evaluative adjectives such as in "typical blonde."

9. Do not assume that only the men or boys or only the women or girls in a group are capable of answering particular types of questions. That is, do not assume that the sex of the members of the group determines their behavior, their knowledge, or their interests.

10. When discussing the contents of articles, files, stories, novels and various kinds of studies, look for any possible sex-related bias in the material and bring these to the attention of the group or try to elicit comments about these biases. For the language or literature teacher, this last area is a particularly rich one as many language and linguistic texts, to say nothing of the stories and novels that surround us, abound in sexist and unfair language examples.

In addition to all of these, there are the many specific suggestions which can be found in one of many guides to non-sexist writing. For those not familiar with such guides, please see the Modern Language Association's Guidelines, those of the American Psychological Association, etc. These are also useful guides for students and would provide good classroom examples.

By setting an example in the classroom, teachers can tangibly demonstrate the vitality of non-sexist language. Obviously, such language need not be awkward, stodgy or "ungrammatical" and may instead be forward-looking and refreshingly inclusive of all individuals addressed. As an in-class exercise, it may in fact prove useful to take various examples from students' journals and open them up for class discussion. That is, not only the details of the language forms need to be attacked and discussed but also the atmosphere communicated by the type of language labeled "sexist."

There are countless examples of sexist language in everyday speech. Most of the examples that we come across are detrimental to women either because they stereotype women negatively or because they render women invisible. I do not intend to suggest that there are no examples of sexist language that diminish men. There are. However, the English language as we know it, as evidenced in particular by the masculine generic and as seen by the social interpretation of many sexually unidentified nominals, views "male" as the norm. By implication, "female" is deviant. Such bias in language is precisely the sort of thing that can contribute to and teach sexist thinking.

As stated at the beginning of this paper, it is my belief that the gender-related language forms that we are exposed to and that we learn as children contribute significantly to our expectations and views of one another as men and women. Language labels our universe for us; it helps us categorize reality and allows us to organize conceptually our world. Since gender distinctions are a major part of that organization, the ways in which (and the degree to which) such word forms influence us is of great importance to language study and furthermore to a general understanding of human thinking. The failure to bring about linguistic change (that is, to eliminate sexism from language) promises to perpetuate the sexist attitudes that are being formed, communicated and constantly reinforced. We have a responsibility to teach this to our students and to aid them in eliminating from their own language what may be for many an unconscious bias.

Notes

1. Research for this paper was supported by an NEH Summer Seminar Grant and by the Career Development Fund of Montclair State College.

2. Some of these ideas were first developed in a paper I delivered at the 1982 Northeast Modern Language Association Meetings, "Sexist Language in the Classroom."

Works Cited

Miller, Casey, and Kate Swift. "One Small Step for Genkind." *New York Times Magazine*, April 16, 1972. 36, 99-101, 106.

Vetterling-Braggin, Mary, Ed. *Sexist Language: A Modern Philosophical Analysis.* Totowa, NJ: Littlefield, Adams, 1981.

Chapter Three

Writing and Speaking:
The Student's Authority

This chapter is concerned with recognizing student authority, a process that begins with valuing the student's personal experience and incorporating it into the classroom. The authors show how teacher-centered writing classes can promote either confrontation or acquiescence, and silence the student's individual voice, whereas a student-centered approach promotes self-esteem, resourcefulness, and peace in the classroom. The essays suggest ways of supplanting tightly controlled, teacher-centered modes, a restructuring that encourages the student to write and speak with authority.

Equity and Peace in the New Writing Class

Olivia Frey

In May, 1984, Peggy McIntosh and Elizabeth Minnich of the Wellesley Center for Research on Women visited St. Olaf and consulted with our faculty about the first drafts of their proposals for a feminist curriculum, "Implications of Women's Studies for the Humanities: A Guidebook for Faculty and Curriculum Development." McIntosh and Minnich suggested what, ideally, the feminist writing pedagogy would be. It occurred to me that they were describing what writing pedagogy, in many cases, actually is. In June, I conducted a seminar on Peace/Justice issues in the English class for the ALC/LCA task force on global education.[1] During the week long seminar, we discussed not only how to teach such works as *The Iliad* and *Three Guineas*, but also what teaching strategies would create the peaceable classroom.[2] It occurred to us that if our advocacy of peace was to have any validity, we could not continue "to do violence" to our students with traditional classroom practices such as grading and the fiercely competitive atmosphere that it encourages. At the same time we discussed some of the more recent methods of teaching writing, seeing many of them as conducive to peace and justice.

My summers are usually for recreation, and this past summer was no different. It was also a time of re-creation, an awakening. As a result of my participation in the two workshops, I have been able to look with a new eye at recent changes in writing instruction, a change from emphasis on the product to emphasis on the process; from concern that writing conform to certain prescribed conventions of correctness to concern that writing be appropriate for the context in which it is written. Research as well as my own experience suggest that this shift in writing instruction has helped teachers to teach better and students to write better. Not until this summer have I realized how much better. The new writing class is not only more effective, but equitable and peaceable as well.

In the rough drafts of their curriculum guide, McIntosh and Minnich describe the ideal writing class, taught from what they consider is the feminist perspective, that should exist in the schools across the country:

What would make possible this ideal relationship of the student to writing and of the instructor to the student? The writer described above is not blocked or terrified, nor deadened, nor divorced from the process of writing. She is intellectually and emotionally limber in the presence of the assignment. She produces writing which the instructor has time and motivation to follow closely. Both are interested, perhaps even enjoying themselves, in the process which feels to the student more like self-development than like "English." The course is student-centered and focused on the student's writing. The teacher acts not as a correcter of bad writing, but as a more experienced co-speaker and co-writer. The instructor has achieved what, in terms of our model of phases, is a Phase IV pedagogy, (14).

The writing classes that McIntosh and Minnich describe do exist. Composition teachers and researchers have anticipated feminists by several years. Maxine Hairston, in "The Winds of Change: Thomas Kuhn and the Revolution in the Teaching of Writing," outlines the dramatic change that has taken place in the last few years in composition pedagogy, a change that she compares to Kuhn's shift in scientific paradigms:

[C]hanges are under way, and the traditional prescriptive and product-centered paradigm that underlies writing instruction is beginning to crumble. Forces contributing to its demise are both theoretical and concrete and come from both inside and outside the profession. Changes in theory probably started, in the middle 1950's, from intellectual inquiry and speculation about language and language learning that was going on in several fields, notably linguistics, anthropology, and clinical and cognitive psychology (4).

Most writing teachers are aware of the substance of these changes, but in order to understand exactly how the "new" writing class conforms to McIntosh's and Minnich's feminist model, or to be more precise, is equitable as well as peaceful, I will explain these changes. In doing so, I generalize quite freely about the "old" and the "new" writing class, keeping at all times in mind Hairston's own *caveat*:

Although those in the vanguard of the profession have by and large adopted the process model for teaching composition and are now attentively watching the research on the composing process in order to extract some pedagogical principles from it, the overwhelming majority of college writing teachers in the United States are not professional writing teachers. They are trained as literary critics first and as teachers of literature second. Yet, out of necessity, most of them are doing half or more of their teaching in composition. And they teach it by the traditional paradigm, just as they did when they were untrained assistants ten or twenty or forty years ago (5).

I was one of those untrained assistants and, until six years ago, taught writing according to the traditional paradigm. We graduate assistants and most of the full-time faculty gave assignments, the students wrote their essays, and we marked their essays, using the correction symbols that correspond to sections in *The Macmillan Handbook of English*. Students "revised" their essays, but revision then hardly resembled what revision is today. In order to keep the grade that they had received, students had to correct the errors that we had marked. Most of the time, they corrected only grammatical errors. We actually discouraged full-scale revising. In making corrections, students supposedly looked up the appropriate section in the handbook that corresponded to the symbol, read the explanation of the rule, checked the sample exercises, and then corrected their essays accordingly. The process was painstaking, for us as well as for the students. There were 23 different comma errors alone. Unlike directors of composition now, the director of composition then was primarily responsible for checking to see that T.A.'s marked student essays thoroughly. In my conferences with the director, I was criticized only if I had missed an error, identified an error incorrectly, or graded too high. We never discussed how to teach writing. And I knew better than to ask why my students seemed to make the same mistakes on essay after essay.

Most of us, T.A.'s and professors alike, marked on, never questioning the assumptions on which this method was based or even its ineffectiveness. We were actually depending on the system of correcting papers to teach writing. We believed that knowledge of grammar and usage would result in good essays, that the lessons students learned correcting one essay would carry over to their subsequent essays. We filled the essays with our marks, assuming they would teach. T.A.'s rarely held conferences, since canceling classes for them was taboo, and we were too busy with our own classes or our dissertations, just as the full-time faculty was preoccupied with publishing, lest they perish. Neither did we talk about writing very much in class, although we did discuss rhetorical techniques or methods of organization, and students plugged in the formulas. Nevertheless, many essays lacked style, grace, substance. Most were boring. There was no room in the plan to encourage students to re-envision their papers or flesh-out their ideas. I used the symbol "awk" too often, a convenient catch-all for too many different kinds of errors. The awkward passages reflected confused thinking and not ignorance of grammar, yet I just couldn't write small enough in the margins of their papers to explain how their thinking had gone wrong.

Not just the correction symbols, but the whole method of teaching writing during those years was profoundly inadequate. Noticing this inadequacy and hoping to improve methods of teaching writing, composition specialists thought that they could learn something by studying how professional writers wrote.[3] Researchers discovered that professional writers rarely worried about their grammar or their spelling, those prescriptive rules that we hoped would enable our students to write better. Professional writers worried, rather, about who would read what they wrote, how to satisfy the expectations of this audience, and about what they themselves were trying to achieve, and whether or not they had successfully done so; these concerns were much more profound, much broader than grammatical correctness. Some professional writers did worry about grammar, but after they had shaped their ideas, given their ideas voice to their satisfaction. They made changes as they went, not with grammar book in hand, but with their audience and purpose in mind. Their intentions determined their choices and the shape of their writing, even the very shape of their sentences.

As composition specialists shared their findings, writing instruction in the class, too, shifted its emphasis from the prescriptive rules in the handbook to the context in which a piece was written—who the audience was, who the writer was, what the writer hoped to accomplish, when it was written, why it was written. Writing instruction also began to accommodate the actual stages of the writing process—by including time for students to generate ideas and revise drafts, even incubate, before turning in a final draft—components of writing instruction that were unheard of according to the old method, either because of unrealistic notions of what students would accomplish on their own or, more likely, the notion that a writer either had it or he or she didn't, either knew the rules or he or she didn't, and a series of drafts would make very little difference. Knowing the rules meant success. Satisfying the instructor meant success. Not much else.

Satisfying the instructor is much less important in the new writing class. The class is less hierarchical and authoritarian. It is student-centered rather than subject-centered or teacher-centered. The teacher no longer has the Truth about writing. The student has the truth as she makes the writing her own. The new writing teacher questions and suggests, but rarely mandates.[4] The teacher is a resource person and a guide. If the teacher imposes a set of prescribed rules on the piece, or rewrites passages according to his standards or taste, the writing is no longer the student's, but the teacher's. The new writing teacher avoids what has come to be termed in the profession "appropriation of the text" (Brannon, Knoblauch, 157-166).

This is not to say that in the new writing class, "anything goes." As Donald Murray writes:

I teach the student not the paper but this doesn't mean I'm a "like wow" teacher. I am critical and I certainly can be directive but I listen before I speak. Most times my students make tough—sometimes too tough— evaluations of their work. I have to curb their too critical eye and help them see what works and what might work so they know how to read evolving writing so it will evolve into writing worth reading (15).

In the new writing class, there are more students like Andrea, a student of Murray's, who "bustles in, late, confused, appearing disorganized." But, according to Murray, she is far from disorganized. She, and not the teacher, is in charge of her writing.

Out comes the clipboard when I pass her paper back to her. She tells me exactly what she attempted to do, precisely where she succeeded and how, then informs me what she intends to do next. She will not work on this draft; she is bored with it. She will go back to an earlier piece, the one I liked and she didn't like. Now she knows what to do with it. She starts to pack up and leave (18).

There are fewer students like those I taught in graduate school, waiting for me to give them the word, learning the rules, making the same mistakes in paper after paper, and, even sadder, never knowing and never caring to know why they were writing.

Having changed in the ways that I suggest, the new writing class cannot help but be more equitable, especially if we consider that in the old class, an essay's success or failure depended on how it conformed to traditional rhetorical or syntactic standards generated out of a cultural, political, or social context that was (and is) largely patriarchal, white, privileged. In the new writing class, a variety of forms, language and subject matter is now appropriate because an essay's success more often depends on the degree to which a writer has achieved her purpose or reached her audience, rather than to what degree the essay conforms to supposedly objective, prescriptive rules.[5]

Indeed, Murray's writing class is fundamentally different from the freshperson composition classes that I taught in graduate school. His classes, like many "new" writing classes, are not classes at all, but conferences. When teachers do hold classes, they barely resemble the old in which the instructor taught writing by lecturing about the semi-colon or talking about essays that illustrated the various rhetorical forms. In the new writing class, teachers often use peer inquiry—students sharing and critiquing each other's writing in pairs or in small groups. As writing has evolved over the years, teachers have used these two pedagogical techniques of conferencing and peer inquiry more and more. Along with the emphasis on process and purpose, these techniques contribute to a more equitable classroom.

The tone and focus of Murray's meeting with Andrea suggest the equitable nature of conferences:

> I feel as if I have been searching for years for the right questions, questions which would establish a tone of master and apprentice, no, the voice of a fellow craftsman having a conversation about a piece of work, writer to writer, neither praise nor criticism but questions which imply further drafts, questions which draw helpful comments out of the student writer.
>
> And now that I have my questions, they quickly become unnecessary. My students ask these questions of themselves before they come to me. They have taken my conferences away from me. They come in and tell me what has gone well, what has gone wrong, and what they intend to do about it (15).

The instructor is more a guide than an authority figure. The student determines the direction of the meeting as well as the direction of her writing. Yet what most makes this method equitable is that the student and instructor can come to know each other. As a result, the student becomes a person rather than a type. It is in the conference that the instructor talks with Andrea, or Shane, or Namoch, a meeting that, better than anything else, will work to dispel misconceptions that the instructor might hold about "women," or "Blacks," or "Asians," unfair generalizations that feed prejudice and injustice in the world outside of the classroom.

For the same reasons, that is, because students meet one another face to face and learn about each other, peer inquiry promotes equity and tolerance. Researchers have on several occasions advocated using "cooperative learning" in order to encourage the successful integration of schools (Cook, 97-113). In small groups, the barriers of "us" and "them" begin to break down. People that students have typed all of a sudden have faces and feelings, individual needs and talents, and weaknesses. The stereotypes no longer fit. Cooperative learning is also more equitable because it is simply that—cooperative. The students succeed as a group; they succeed because they cooperate rather than because they compete. They learn that one's achievement does not always depend on another's failure.

What makes the new writing class equitable also makes it peaceable. The pedagogical techniques of peer inquiry especially encourages understanding and cooperation, infertile ground for aggression. To say that such a method fosters peace does not mean that conflicts never arise. Conflict occurs often. Group work and peer inquiry, nevertheless, discourage harmful confrontation since through cooperative learning students discover how to resolve conflict creatively and effectively. Arguments, verbal violence, and, finally, physical violence are spawned by resourcefulness, and small groups enrich the students' store of resources for living and working with others.

Resourcefulness, helplessness, frustration are all akin, and their horrible offspring is violence.[6] While overt violence in the classroom is rare, the adversarial relationship between teacher and student that we too often find in the traditional classroom contains these seeds of violence. In too many old writing classes, the student perceived the teacher as the judge on the side of the system, upholding the rules even at the expense of the student. In such a situation, the student does not really engage in learning, but succeeds academically by conforming or acquiescing. Students write correct papers in order to complete assignments. They do not write because it is pleasurable or gratifying. The act of writing rarely becomes their own, to use to satisfy their needs or discover themselves or their world. As a result, many do not write very well. And it has nothing to do with grammar.

The suppression of students' intrinsic needs as writers, like other more obvious forms of oppression, is a type of violence, even if it is inadvertent because of the structure of the class or the pedagogy that we use. Although we never raise a hand, we do violence to our students, and they do violence to themselves. In the new peaceable writing class, however, the teacher is a guide encouraging discovery and not a judge mandating conformity. The instructor's evaluations rarely seem arbitrary since the teacher and student have worked together at every stage of the essay. Students fail less often since the act of writing means more to them, and their goals are clearer. Also, with peer inquiry and conferencing, students receive more guidance along the way. If students do fail, they certainly do not fail in the usual sense, feeling humiliated, confused, angry. They more often learn from their mistakes. They learn resilience, tenacity, self-esteem, resourcefulness. They learn peace.

After all I have said, the learning situation seems ideal. But believe it or not, students feel, at least at first, extremely uncomfortable in the new writing class. It is easier to write by following a formula, abiding by prescribed, predetermined standards. *Not* writing according to formula requires that the writer make choices at every stage. The writer, not the teacher, chooses a topic; the writer decides the shape and length of her essay as well as the rhetorical strategies that she will use; the writer decides whether or not her words are appropriate. Students are unaccustomed to and uncomfortable with having to make so many choices, and composition writers especially cling to any maxim that the writing teacher offers, grasping at rules as the key to good writing. But after the initial frustration and insecurity, students develop resourcefulness, a trait not only conducive to peace, but essential for awareness and growth of the feminine Self.

Resourcefulness is the ability to make judgments, to assess situations, to use one's mind and experiences, in short, to use one's own inner resources to make decisions and act, or not to act, to be, to become. Any person who lacks these inner resources is more likely to conform or to lash out. A woman who lacks these inner resources looks to an outside world for a definition of herself and shapes her being accordingly. In small ways, the new writing class encourages a woman to develop her inner resources. She must make choices, discover her purpose as a writer, shape her writing according to her own needs, and justify *to herself first* the choices she has made and the writing she has created. To do all of this, she must depend on her mind, her resources, and she must be honest, or her writing will reflect her dependence or resourcefulness. Uncertainty makes itself known in garbled syntax. Dishonesty manifests itself in ambiguous pronoun reference or the overused passive. The writing tells.

As the student makes small choices, then important ones, she discovers her rhetorical voice along with her personal, female voice. In Gilbert and Gubar's terms, in *The Madwoman in the Attic*, the new writing class recovers the authority of the writer's own experience. The "patriarchal definition," in this case prescriptive rhetoric and grammar, no longer "intervene between herself and herself," between the image in the mirror that society has created, and the genuine self behind the mask (17). While writing in the old class is reduced to a skill, in the new class it becomes an act of creation in the most profound sense, not only of words, but of a peaceful world and of a new woman.

Notes

1. The Division of Colleges and University Services of the American Lutheran Church and the Department of Higher Education of the Lutheran Church in America, Summer Institute on Global Studies, Augsburg College, Minneapolis, Minnesota, June 10-15, 1984.

2. In our seminar, we used as a starting point for discussion Mary Rose O'Reilly's "The Peaceable Classroom," *College English* 46 (February 1984): 103-112.

3. It is impossible to list all of the research and publications that have propelled the revolution in writing instruction. Nevertheless, I would like to suggest reading the following works, considered instrumental in changing the course of writing instruction in this country: James Britton, Anthony Burgess, Nancy Martin, Alex McLeod, and Harold Rosen, *The Development of Writing Abilities 11-18*, MacMillan Research Series, (London: MacMillan Education, 1975); Janet Emig, *The Composing Processes of Twelfth Graders* (Urbana, IL: Na-

tional Council of Teachers of English, 1971); Linda S. Flower and John R. Hayes, "A Cognitive Process Theory of Writing," *College Composition and Communication* 35 (December 1981): 365-387; W. Labov, *The Study of Non-Standard English* (Urbana, IL: National Council of Teachers of English, 1970); James Moffett, *Teaching the Universe of Discourse* (New York: Houghton Mifflin, 1968); Sondra Perl, "The Composing Process of Unskilled College Writers," *Research in the Teaching of English* 13 (December 1979): 317-336; Mina P. Shaughnessy, *Errors and Expectations* (New York: Oxford University Press, 1977); Nancy Somers, "Revision Strategies of Student Writer and Experienced Adult Writers," *College Composition and Communication* 31 (December 1980): 378-388.

4. How teachers mark compositions has changed dramatically since I was a teaching assistant. Rather than marking up a paper with cryptic correction symbols, the teacher more often asks questions, makes suggestions, or records immediate responses. According to Nina Ziv, comments on essays "can only be helpful if teachers respond to student writing as part of an ongoing dialogue between themselves and their students. In order to create such a dialogue, teachers might begin by responding to student writing not as evaluators and judges but as interested adults would react to such writing." Nina D. Ziv, "The Effect of Teacher Comments on the Writing of Four College Freshmen," *New Directions in Composition Research*, Eds. Richard Beach and Lillian S. Bridwell (New York: The Guilford Press, 1984).

5. I would also like to suggest that the same attitude that has changed composition pedagogy, an attitude that is in the broadest sense an altered perspective on what constitutes legitimate discourse, has encouraged the discipline of literary studies as a whole to reconsider the canon. For example, the diary or narrative is a mode of discourse in which women have often chosen to express themselves. The mode is internal, personal, concrete, in many ways an inherently "female" form, if we are to take Carol Gilligan's observations seriously. It is not surprising, nevertheless, that such writing has been considered out of the mainstream since, according to the traditional and

perhaps outmoded rhetorical standards, exposition or argument is the "highest" form of discourse, while narrative or description is the "lowest."

6. See, for example, Sigmund Freud, *Civilization and Its Discontents* (London: Hogarth Press, 1930); Erich Fromm, *The Anatomy of Human Destructiveness* (New York: Holt, Rinehart and Winston, 1973); Irenaus Eibl-Eibesfeldt, *The Biology of Peace and War* (New York: The Viking Press, 1979); Konrad Lorenz, *On Aggression* (New York: Harcourt, Brace and World, 1966); M. F. Ashley Montagu, Ed., *Man and Aggression* (New York: Oxford University Press, 1968); M. F. Ashley Montagu, *The Nature of Human Aggression* (New York: Oxford University Press, 1976); and Natalie Shainess, *Sweet Suffering: Woman As Victim* (New York: The Bobbs-Merrill Co., Inc., 1984). Lorenz, Freud and Eibl-Eibesfeldt assert that aggression is innate; Montagu, Fromm and Shainess that it is learned and not inevitable. All agree that resourcefulness results in violence, that aggression, innate or learned, need not result in destruction or murder.

Works Cited

Brannon, Lil, and C. H. Knoblauch. "On Students' Rights to Their Own Texts: A Model of Teacher Response." *College Composition and Communication* 33 (May 1982): 157-166.

Cook, Stuart W. "Interpersonal and Attitudinal Outcomes in Cooperating Interracial Groups." *Journal of Research and Development in Education*. 12, No. 1 (Fall 1978): 97-113.

Gilbert, Sandra M. and Susan Gubar. *The Madwoman in the Attic: The Woman Writer and the Nineteenth-Century Literary Imagination*. New Haven, CT: Yale University Press, 1979.

Hairston, Maxine. "The Winds of Change: Thomas Kuhn and the Revolution in Teaching Writing." *Current Issues in Higher Education: Writing Across Curriculum*. American Association for Higher Education, No. 3 (1983-84): 4-10.

McIntosh, Peggy, and Elizabeth Minnich. "Implication of

Women's Studies for the Humanities: A Guidebook for Faculty and Curriculum Development." Unpublished manuscript.

Murray, Donald M. "The Listening Eye: Reflections on the Writing Conference." *College English* 41 (September 1979): 13-18.

Gender, Race, and Class: In Quest of the Perfect Writing Theme

Diana J. Fuss

My quest for the perfect writing theme began a year ago when I received the fateful news that I would be teaching English 1 — "The Process of Writing" — to twenty-one Brown University first-year students mandated (by the Dean of the College, no less) to enroll in a composition course none of them wished to take. The scenario is a familiar one to any writing instructor faced with the seemingly monumental task of teaching a resistant, perhaps even openly hostile, class the fundamentals of composing readable prose. How, we wonder in silent despair, can we possibly capture the imagination and motivation of students who not only come to us from various academic disciplines within the university, but also from widely divergent personal backgrounds? What composition theme could possibly draw such a diverse audience together and still succeed in addressing the academic and personal needs of each individual student?

Obviously, we can arrive at no easy answers to a problem which has vexed writing teachers for longer than any of us care to admit. Yet I think it is a mistake simply to shrug our shoulders and select a course theme blindly, hoping for the best; certain course themes do have a better success rate than others, often regardless of who teaches the course. What I propose to do here is first examine, in a theoretical fashion, exactly what factors contribute to a successful course theme; second, I intend to use the theme "Gender, Race, and Class" to demonstrate, in a more concrete way, how these factors operate within the specific context of a writing course.

One particularly important factor that any writing instructor must keep in mind is the actual, pragmatic needs of the students who enroll in her class. Students frequently complain that writing courses offered by the English department are really literature courses in disguise; instructors, they tell us, spend more class time lecturing on individual works of literature than on addressing their more urgent writing needs. Science majors frequently bemoan learning how to write a literary explication of a poem when what they really need to learn is how to write up the results of their scientific research; similarly, pre-law concentrators find assignments which stress personal and reflective responses to literature quite useless in a field which demands more persuasive and argumentative prose. Different academic disciplines demand different kinds of writing, and so I find it difficult not to sympathize with those students who come to us hoping to learn the codes and conventions of the literature in their own chosen fields only to leave our department frustrated and confused.

A writing theme, above all, should be expansive enough to incorporate the exigencies posed by any field of study in any part of the university curriculum. When we choose composition themes exclusively from our own areas of expertise, we may satisfy our personal interests and our need to feel secure about the body of information we teach, but we also may achieve this confidence at the cost of denying our students an opportunity to learn about other modes of writing which may be more useful in their personal and academic growth. The issue can be a touchy one since we all prefer to believe that what fascinates us personally and professionally must also intrigue our students, and that what students learn in writing about English literature also applies to their writing in other courses; but as teachers of writing—not necessarily teachers of literature—I believe we have a responsibility to meet the students' needs as we find them, not as we create them. Writing courses with themes like "The Motif of Love and Death in American Poetry" or even "Gender Roles in Contemporary British Fiction" may not, in fact, serve as appropriate subject matter for teaching students the actual process of writing. I am reminded here of Erika Lindemann's helpful distinction, posed in *A Rhetoric for Writing Teachers*, between a "what-centered" course and a "how-centered" course: a "what-centered" course emphasizes the subject matter of writing, whereas a "how-centered" course focuses on the process students engage in when they compose on any topic (242-244). The great advantage of the "how-centered" course over the "what-centered" course is that it shifts our pedagogical focus away from strict subject matter and turns our attention towards students actually involved in the practice of writing.

As appealing as this process model sounds, we need to remind ourselves that students still must write *about* something; no one can compose in a vacuum, least of all a beginning or inexperienced writer. We come back then to the problem of theme and the challenge of creating a course which will meet the particular needs of each of the many students enrolled. At the risk of setting down dangerous prescriptions, let me offer three very general guidelines which I believe may prove particularly helpful in designing feasible themes for composition classes: first, a writing theme should be broad enough to allow students considerable latitude in choosing their specific paper topics while still pointing them in a general direction; second, a theme should not exclude any writer by positing as a prerequisite a given field of knowledge (such as literary analysis) which the student may not be familiar with nor have the time and leisure to learn; and third, a theme should be flexible enough to prove workable for any student, no matter what the writer's previous experience and ability.

Let me demonstrate the practical appeal of each of these guidelines with one of my own (and my students') favorite course themes: "Gender, Race, and Class." Perhaps the greatest problem we face as writing instructors is finding topics which each student can feel comfortable writing about— topics which allow novice writers to build on some small area of expertise and which help them to gain the confidence they need to branch out into new areas of discovery. Happily, all students find themselves experts in fields of gender, race, and class. Unlike writing themes which rely wholly on an outside body of knowledge which many students fail to possess, "Gender, Race, and Class" taps the varied and unique personal experiences of the students while still suggesting larger fields of inquiry they may wish to pursue in their writing. The experiential component provides the impetus for a more academic examination of three factors which play such a crucial role in shaping all our lives; the personal neatly meshes with the political, demonstrating to the student writer, in a very concrete and direct fashion, the impossibility of separating the two.

In addition to underscoring the vital relationship between experiential and academic ways of knowing, a theme as broad as the one I propose lends itself easily to an interdisciplinary approach to the teaching of writing. For example, students majoring in biology or mathematics can easily embark upon a scientific study of sexual, racial, and economic issues; students interested in sociology or philosophy can learn a social sciences approach to the course theme; and students involved in music or foreign languages can approach the course from a humanities perspective. Some students may even wish to dabble in all three traditional areas of study, learning the various prose conventions appropriate for different types of academic papers as they continue to develop and polish their own writing style. An interdisciplinary approach to the teachers of composition becomes particularly important as university departments, like the business communities which surround them, become increasingly specialized and students are expected to compose so many different types of discourses for so many different kinds of situations. Perhaps we can provide our students with the greatest service by teaching them how to compose different kinds of papers; by showing them how to adapt their tone, diction, and style to a given audience and situation; and, finally, by providing them with a course theme which will allow them to accomplish these goals within an interdisciplinary framework.

A flexible theme like "Gender, Race, and Class" poses a third possibility for the teaching of composition: it allows us to facilitate the progress of individual students by offering them writing material that is within their cognitive grasp and yet still poses a challenge to their intellect. As we all know

from experience, in virtually any writing course we find ourselves teaching student writers so diverse in their writing abilities and educational backgrounds that we hardly know which
audience to choose for our own spoken and written discourses.
I see no convenient solution to this perplexing pedagogical
problem, although with a theme as broad as "Gender, Race,
and Class," the students at least can be confident that the subject matter itself is accessible to all of them and excludes no
one on the basis of ability or knowledge. Moreover, students
can explore other interests under the general thematic heading: a writer who finds the topic of gender uninteresting may
find the subject of class more to her liking; or a writer who
finds religion an all-consuming passion can deepen and expand
his field of interest by exploring the role of women in the
church or the problem of slavery in the *Old Testament.* The
possibilities seem endless. Finally, the actual title "Gender,
Race, and Class" poses fewer anxieties for male students so
often frightened away by feminist approaches to learning, or
white students who ignore Afro-American, Asian, or Third
World courses at their peril, or even upper-class students who
persistently shy away from Marxist approaches to literature
and culture. "Gender, Race, and Class" is just inclusive
enough to be pragmatically useful to both teacher and student
engaged in the mutual process of learning.

I should note, in closing, that a writing course which takes as
its very theme questions of equity and justice brings with it a
considerable bonus prize. As teachers we have the responsibility to educate not just our students' minds but their sensibilities as well, and perhaps no greater challenge exists for us than
to break down the cultural barriers which spawn ignorance and
prejudice and which thereby impede the educational process.
Certainly, my own experience in teaching a composition
course centered on the interrelated issues of sexual, racial, and
economic difference has not been without its problems. Specifically, I discovered early in the course that students, given a
choice between the three major topics, inevitably shied away
from those very subjects which threatened them the most: in
general, white students avoided the issue of race, male students ignored questions of gender, and foreign students (curi-

Creation and Relation: Teaching Essays By T. S. Eliot and Adrienne Rich

Mary DeShazer

"The more perfect the artist, the more completely separate in him
will be the man who suffers and the mind which creates" (54).
　　T. S. Eliot, "Tradition and the Individual Talent"
"There must be ways, and we will be finding out more and more
about them, in which the energy of creation and the energy of relation
can be united" (43).
　　Adrienne Rich, " 'When We Dead Awaken': Writing as Re-Vision"

What is, and what should be, the role of writing in the modern
age? What relationship exists between contemporary writing
and that of the past? To what extent should personal experience and emotions "invade" a writer's work? These and related
literary and rhetorical concerns provide the subject matter of
T. S. Eliot's classic essay "Tradition and the Individual Talent"
and Adrienne Rich's soon-to-be-classic " 'When We Dead
Awaken': Writing as Re-Vision." Since Eliot's answers to these
questions reflect a traditional "masculinist" perspective while
Rich's offer a radical feminist vision, these two essays can be
used effectively in the composition classroom, both as models
for rhetorical analysis and as a means of introducing students
to links between feminism and the practice and evaluation of
writing.

In my advanced rhetoric course, our analysis of Eliot's and
Rich's artistic philosophies begins with the key terms on
which each essay pivots. For Eliot, this term is "tradition," a
concept whose understanding, he claims, is "nearly indispensable" to anyone other than the most youthful and amateurish

of writers. Tradition "cannot be inherited," Eliot explains, "and if you want it you must obtain it by great labour." It involves "the historical sense," an awareness of both the "pastness" and the "presence" of the past:

The historical sense compels a man to write not merely with his own generation in his bones, but with a feeling that the whole of the literature of Europe from Homer and within it the whole of the literature of his own country has a simultaneous existence and composes a simultaneous order (49).

No writer, Eliot continues, "no artist of any art, has his complete meaning alone....You cannot value him alone; you must set him, for contrast and comparison, among the dead." As a principle of aesthetic criticism, then, this emphasis on tradition leads Eliot to praise most highly that writing which takes its place among an already existing "ideal order," altering this order "ever so slightly" but essentially conforming to preexistent norms. Both the writer-initiate and that writer's works "must inevitably be judged by the standards of the past" (Eliot, 49-50).

It is of course significant that Eliot's aspiring author is a "man," a generic "he" whose central creative task is to complement the endeavors of his ancestors—those male forerunners whom Harold Bloom has labeled "precursors." For Adrienne Rich, in contrast, the incipient writers under discussion are women, "sleepwalkers" awakening at last to a "collective reality," a sexual and political world view which will inevitably affect the purpose and nature of their artistic efforts. For contemporary women, Rich asserts, writing demands "re-vision":

Re-vision—the act of looking back, of seeing with fresh eyes, of entering an old text from a new critical direction—is for women more than a chapter in cultural history: it is an act of survival. Until we can understand the assumptions in which we are drenched we cannot know ourselves. . . . We need to know the writing of the past, and know it differently than we have ever known it, not to pass on a tradition but to break its hold over us (35).

"Tradition" is a dangerous concept for women writers, Rich concludes, because the artistic standards it promotes purport to be "universal" but actually are male-centered, male-defined. To "re-vision" this masculinist aesthetic requires a radical feminist critique which "would take the work first of all as a clue to how we live, how we have been living, how we have been led to imagine ourselves, how our language has trapped as well as liberated us, how the very act of naming has been until now a male prerogative, and how we can begin to see and name—and therefore live—afresh" (Rich, 35).

If Eliot and Rich disagree about the value of tradition and the writer's relationship to the past, they also view differently the concepts of artistic methodology and voice. Eliot offers an "impersonal theory" of writing, one which advocates objectivity, separation, detachment. Only the "bad writer" becomes "personal," he claims, for the more perfect the artist, the more distance there will be between the "man who suffers" and the "mind which creates." The "minds" of Europe, of the United States, of other people are more important than the writer's own mind, Eliot answers, because the creative process involves "dehumanization": "a continual self-sacrifice, a continual extinction of personality" (53). Good writing, then, "is not a turning loose of emotion, but an escape from emotion; it is not the expression of a personality, but an escape from personality" (58).

Rich, on the other hand, believes that the best writing by women today challenges this philosophy of dehumanization; it is subjective, engaged, attached. If a work is to "coalesce," she argues,

there has to be an imaginative transformation of reality which is in no way passive. . . . Moreover, if the imagination is to transcend and transform experience it has to question, to challenge, to conceive of alternatives . . . nothing can be too sacred for the imagination to turn into its opposite or to call experimentally by another name. For writing is re-naming. (43).

The woman writer "re-names" by casting off the shackles of tradition, by rejecting what Rich deems "the myth of the masculine artist and thinker": the belief that to write well one must "become unavailable to others . . . a devouring ego" (43). Instead, women writers must explore ways of combining the "energy of creation" and the "energy of relation" (43). Rather than extinguishing her personality and life experience, as Eliot advocates, Rich's creative woman must acknowledge that it is "the woman's sense of *herself*—embattled, possessed" that gives her work "its dynamic charge, its rhythms of struggle, need, will, and female energy" (36).

For whom is good writing written and what is its ultimate goal? On these issues, too, Eliot and Rich offer divergent perspectives. Eliot's "ideal reader" is, by his own admission, over twenty-five, male, and erudite. Although he acknowledges that his "programme for the *metier*" of writing may be criticized for its "pedantry," Eliot argues adamantly that the good writer must seek erudition. "Some can absorb knowledge," he explains archly, "the more tardy must sweat for it" (52). In defending the "dehumanization" of art he is similarly firm: only those readers "who have personality and emotions know what it means to want to escape from these things" (58). For Rich, in contrast, all traditional assumptions about audience should be called into question by the woman writer:

No male writer has written primarily or even largely for women, or with the sense of women's criticism as a consideration when he chooses his materials, his theme, his language. But to a lesser or greater extent, every woman writer has written for men even when . . . she was supposed to be addressing women. If we have come to the point when this balance might begin to change, when women can stop being haunted, not only by "convention and propriety" but by internalized fears of being and saying themselves, then it is an extraordinary moment for the woman writer—and reader (37-38).

In regard to purpose, Eliot asserts that the writer's "business" is "to preserve tradition," to create "conformity between the old and the new" (50) subjects and styles of writing. Only the "eccentric" creator seeks "new human emotions to express"; in fact, he warns, any such search will lead invariably to "the perverse." The nature and source of this perversion is never

clearly defined, but Eliot concludes his essay with a grave assessment of the danger of emotional experimentation in art:

The business (of the writer) is not to find new emotion, but to use the
ordinary ones and, in working them up . . . to express feelings which
are not in actual emotions at all. And emotions which he has never
experienced will serve his turn as well as those familiar to him (59).

"The emotion of art is impersonal," he claims finally. The
good writer "cannot reach this impersonality without surren-
dering himself wholly to the work to be done. And he is not
likely to know what is to be done unless he lives in what is
not merely the present, but the present moment of the past"
(58-59).

For women writing today, Rich argues, the expressing of
"new human emotions" is vital, since before them lies the
challenge and promise of "a whole new psychic geography to
be explored." Although this incipient feminist process can be
"exhilarating," she alleges, it is also "a difficult and dangerous
walking on the ice, as we try to find language and images for a
consciousness we are just coming into, and with little in the
past to support us" (35). Yet seeking the "new emotions" that
Eliot renounces is essential for those who would "re-vision"
the modernist aesthetic he represents. Because the "creative
energy of patriarchy is fast running out," Rich asserts, a "new
generation" of women writers is rejecting as false the stand of
"objectivity," that "detachment that would make us sound
more like Jane Austen or Shakespeare." Instead, many women
are exploring and expressing their "refusal to be a victim,"
their long-repressed anger, their "newly released courage to
name, to love each other, to share risk and grief and celebra-
tion." They are writing

out of the psychic energy released when women begin to move out towards what the feminist philosopher Mary Daly has described as the
"new space" on the boundaries of patriarchy (49).

After examining Eliot's and Rich's creative theories, my students and I analyze rhetorically each writer's prose style. "Do

they practice what they preach?" a bemused student once
queried, and further investigation revealed that they do, at
least in these two essays. Eliot's style is formal, his manner detached, at times pontifical; his assertions tend to be absolute:
"no poet, no artist of any art, has his complete meaning alone"
(49). The verbs he most often uses are "is," "cannot," and
"must be"; a favorite adverb is "inevitably." In his desire to assert his point with authority, he sometimes verges on the re-
dundant: "But the difference between art and the event is *always absolute*" (56, my italics). At various points he describes
"errors" of eccentricity, the "wrong places" to seek creative inspiration, the proper "business" of the writer, the place in writing for "*significant* emotion" ("insignificant" emotion remains undefined). Rich's style, on the other hand, is informal,
impassioned, at times vulnerable, always forthright: "I have
hesitated to do what I am going to do now, which is to use
myself as an illustration. For one thing, it's a lot easier and less
dangerous to talk about other women writers" (38). Frequently
chosen verb phrases in Rich's essay are "seems to be," "I
think," and "tends to be"; recurring adverbs include the quali-
fiers "largely," "often," and "almost always." Such generalizations are not without exception, of course. Rich, for example,
uses absolute language in her call for "re-vision" ("A change
. . . is essential") and in her final argument: "the creative energy of patriarchy is fast running out; what remains is its self-
generating energy for destruction" (Rich, 35, 49). And Eliot
offers an occasional qualification or disclaimer ("of course this
is not quite the whole story") (58). Furthermore, it is only fair
to note that Eliot's formal and authoritative tone reflects the
prevailing rhetorical mode of his time. For the most part,
though, Eliot manages to "extinguish" personality in his essay,
while Rich insists on revealing "*herself*—embattled, possessed" (Rich, 36).

These two writers also differ in their strategic use of definitions and analogies. Eliot introduces his central concept, tradition, by exploring how the term is typically misused: "we cannot refer to 'the tradition' or 'a tradition'; at most, we employ
the adjective in saying that the poetry of So-and-so is 'traditional' or even 'too traditional'" (17). It is a mistake, he contin-

ues, either to define tradition as a "phrase of censure" or to let
it remain "vaguely approbative"; its true meaning as an aesthetic concept must be clarified, dissected, re-claimed—as
Eliot proceeds to do in the remainder of the essay. Rich too begins with a key definition, but she explains at once what "re-
vision" is, not what it is not: "the act of looking back, of seeing
with fresh eyes . . . an act of survival" (35). Only later in the essay, as her main argument unfolds, does she mention philosophical and rhetorical concepts anti-thetical to re-vision
("misnaming" as opposed to "re-naming," for instance). Furthermore, both Eliot and Rich describe the writer's mind via
analogies, but of a very different sort. Eliot's "impersonal theory" requires a scientific analogue: "I shall, therefore, invite
you to consider . . . the action which takes place when a bit of
finely filiated platinum is introduced into a chamber con-
taining oxygen and sulphur dioxide." The subsequent catalytic
process, Eliot explains, parallels the act of written creation:
"the mind of the poet is the shred of platinum" (53-54). Rich's
analogy, in contrast, comes from the world of power and adventure. A writer, she argues, must experience an "imaginative
transformation of reality which is in no way passive . . . a certain freedom of the mind"—the freedom to "press on, to enter
the currents of your thought like a glider pilot, knowing that
your motion can be sustained, that the buoyancy of your attention will not be suddenly snatched away" (43).

Such stylistic examination could continue *ad infinitum*. My
students and I have also compared, for example, Eliot's use of
classical literary allusions (Homer, Dante, Shakespeare—all
male figures) with Rich's choice of more contemporary references (Virginia Woolf, Jane Harrison, Sylvia Plath—mostly
female). Consulting Winston Weathers' essay on the "rhetoric
of the series," we have analyzed Eliot's use of balanced phras-
ing, of "two's" ("not only . . . but also"; "poetry is not a turning
loose of emotion, but an escape from emotion") (58), as it con-
trasts with Rich's propensity for series of three's ("guides,
maps, possibilities") and for the longer catalogue (woman "has
served as the painter's model and the poet's muse . . . as com-
forter, nurse, cook, bearer of his seed, secretarial assistant, and
copyist of manuscript") (36). Often we suggest reasons why

Eliot denigrates a "semi-ethical criterion of 'sublimity'" as a means of explaining and evaluating art, and reasons why Rich, though certainly wary of "sublimity," embraces feminism and hence a feminist theory of creativity as "an ethics, a methodology." Juxtaposing the rhetoric and philosophies of Eliot and Rich helps students to appreciate more fully these two essays; it also helps them acquire the skills to analyze the "hidden agendas" in their own stylistic choices.

I have found that advanced composition students relish comparing and contrasting the styles, strategies, and writing theories of Eliot and Rich, and that our classroom activities and discussions generate excellent and varied student work. Since students tend to line up on one side or other (usually, alas, according to gender), oral and written debates abound ("Eliot vs. Rich: What is Good Writing?"). These essays provoke often volatile discussion of the merits and demerits of using the generic "he," of Eliot's assumption that the aspiring writer is male and Rich's equally crisp insistence that she can be and often is female. Personal responses to these debates, and journal entries by students evaluating their own writing according to Rich's or Eliot's standards, are often moving and enlightening. Eliot's theory of impersonality reinforces and elucidates the dogma many composition students have long heard but rarely understood: that truly excellent writing avoids the first-person pronoun, that "I" is to be shunned in favor of a detached persona, someone who "could be" the self but, fortunately, is not. On the other hand, Rich's assessment of good writing may add sanction and legitimacy to efforts by those students who wish to reveal rather than conceal the self in their writing. Frequently students write effective enthymemic arguments supporting or countering either Eliot's traditional or Rich's feministic thesis, or they develop insightful comparisons of poems by these two writers ("J. Alfred Prufrock and Elvira Shatayev: Their Quests to Name the Self"). Such assignments help aspiring writers to evaluate their own rhetorical skills and methods, as well as to examine traditional and nontraditional attitudes toward what makes writing excellent.

My students and I have concluded that what Eliot and Rich disagree on, fundamentally, is the nature and art of rhetoric. By the time we read these essays, we have studied at length what Maxine Hairston calls the "rhetorical square": that interfacing of purpose, method of presentation, speaker, and audience which constitutes effective exposition and argumentation. Using Hairston's paradigm, we have determined through debate and rhetorical analysis that Eliot's major purpose is to extol "tradition" as the ultimate arbiter of excellence in writing, and thus to affirm and to protect a patriarchal aesthetic that he considers inviolable (though perhaps endangered). Rich's goal is precisely the opposite: to break the hold of this tradition over beginning writers, especially women, who often experience the trauma of what feminist critic Suzanne Juhasz has called a "double bind"—a struggle to be both *woman* and *writer* in a society which typically has considered these terms contradictory (1-5). Eliot argues for objectivity in writing, detachment of speaker from subject matter, the use of the persona and the "objective correlative"; Rich praises subjectivity, involvement between writer and content, honest dialogue between speaker/self and audience/selves. Thus they offer two distinct positions on the writer's methodology, voice, and audience. Without renouncing Eliot's argument altogether, I explain my belief as a feminist educator that many teachers, and therefore many generations of students, have been taught to accept without question Eliot's impersonal theory of writing as the only legitimate one. At the very least, I argue, Rich presents both women and men with a stimulating and potentially empowering alternative.

Notes

1. I would like to thank Marilyn Farwell of the University of Oregon for first calling my attention to parallels between Eliot's and Rich's essays.

Works Cited

Bloom, Harold. *The Anxiety of Influence: A Theory of Poetry.* New York: Oxford University Press, 1973.

Eliot, T. S. "Tradition and the Individual Talent." *The Sacred Wood: Essays on Poetry and Criticism.* London: Methuen and Company, Ltd., 1960. 47-59.

Hairston, Maxine. *A Contemporary Rhetoric.* Boston: Houghton Mifflin Co., 1974.

Juhasz, Suzanne. *Naked and Fiery Forms: Modern American Poetry by Women, A New Tradition.* New York: Harper and Row, 1976.

Rich, Adrienne. "'When We Dead Awaken': Writing as Re-Vision." *On Lies, Secrets, and Silence: Selected Prose 1966-1978.* New York: W. W. Norton and Co., 1979. 33-49.

Weathers, Winston. "The Rhetoric of the Series." *Contemporary Essays on Style: Rhetoric, Linguistics, Criticism.* Eds. Glen A. Love and Michael Payne. Glenview, IL: Scott, Foresman and Co., 1969. 21-27.

Teaching Digression as a Mode of Discovery; A Student-Centered Approach to the Discussion of Literature

Mary A. Quinn

Late in *The Catcher in the Rye* Holden Caulfield offers his opinion about digression in the classroom:

> ... lots of times you don't *know* what interests you most till you start talking about something that doesn't interest you most. I mean you can't help it sometimes. What I think is, you're supposed to leave somebody alone if he's at least being interested and he's getting all excited about something. It's nice. You just don't know this teacher, Mr. Vinson. He could drive you crazy sometimes, him and the goddamn class. I mean he'd keep telling you to *unify* and *simplify* all the time. Some things you just can't *do* that to. I mean you can't hardly simplify and unify something just because somebody *wants* you to (Salinger, 184).

For thirty years English teachers have been smiling when they read Holden's assertion (and probably agreeing with him), but how many have actually honored students' digressions in class discussions and writing? During my first year as an instructor in a large literature and composition program, I, like Mr. Vinson, worked hard at guiding students to unify and clarify their essays (for most inexperienced writers "clarify" is synonymous with "simplify"). Because I was teaching in a college program in which writing about literature rather than anything else was expected, I assigned the conventional critical analysis paper. To prepare students for this type of writing, I lectured on relevant matters, and we then discussed in depth whatever literary work we were reading.

Predictably, my students completed their ten-week stint of English Composition doing somewhat more effectively what they had already been practicing throughout high school: they could unify and simplify "like mad." Most students were polite, dutiful, and eager to write what *I* wanted. They were also too often bored and boring. So was I. Of course, they were not at fault, I was; but I did not realize this for several years. After reading several thousand essays that students had painstakingly unified and clarified according to my assiduous instructions, I began to despair. A career of variations on this pedagogical process would be slow but inevitable self-destruction. I was not yet studying the effects of such instruction on my students.

Seldom having been one to challenge the "elders," and having limited confidence in myself as a new teacher, I tentatively and surreptitiously sought alternatives to the traditional approach to writing instruction. The composition information explosion had barely begun, but I read Elbow, Coles, Moffett, Macrorie, and Murray—teachers then regarded as pariahs by many in the lit-comp establishment.[1] One cannot read the work of these people, and the many others now writing in the field of composition studies, without rethinking one's approach not only to writing instruction but also to the entire enterprise of education. As a result of my acquaintance with these writers and, shortly thereafter, my participation in one of the National Writing Project's regional summer institutes in composition, I started reexamining my position as a teacher.[2] I introduced journals into my courses, crude versions of what have since evolved into complex, effective learning logs—fine occasions for written digression (Berthoff, 45-46; Brannon, 56-75; Kirby, 45-57; Fulwiler, 15-31). I then experimented with heuristic procedures such as clustering, mapping, freewriting, and the like, all of which are also preliminary writing activities which foster free association and digression (Rico, 4-19; Murray, *Write to Learn*, 17-33; Winterowd, 55-99; Elbow, *Writing Without Teachers*, 265-269). In time, I came to playing the entire scale: writing response groups, peer editing, read-around groups, and the numerous other effective strategies which teachers have taught other teachers became part of my regular composition repertoire (Healy, 159-162; Elbow, *Writing Without Teachers*, 76-116; Moffett, *Active Voice*, passim; Koch, 85-87).

My liberation as a teacher is such a familiar story in these times that you can easily infer where I now stand on key issues of composition pedagogy—out in the badlands with the thousands of other teachers who make up this new breed. The wealth of excellent information on writing theory and practice now available to teachers in all disciplines, and the number of support systems to which teachers can turn if they wish to continue their education in composition studies, make it difficult for all of us *not* to notice and *not* to participate in the challenging, helpful dialogue about what we do in our classes, whatever our subjects. I leave discussion of teaching writing as a process to those many teachers and researchers who continue expertly to examine and debate issues in this complex field.

Revision of my approach to writing instruction has been accompanied by revision of my ideas about class discussion. My highly structured, teacher-centered lectures and discussion have given way to relatively informal, digressive, student-centered discussion. Only rarely do I lecture, and when I do it is often impromptu. With this second revision in mind, I wish to backtrack from my students' process of writing about literature (assuming one teaches literature and students write about the works they read) in order to focus on class discussion of that literature. For the sake of clarity, allow me to simplify what is actually a complex process: I refer to the sequence of reading-discussion-writing as linear because, unlike the writing process in isolation (which is recursive), we generally ask students first to read a work, then to discuss it, and finally to write about it.[3]

To lead into my thoughts about the importance of digressive discussion as the core of student-centered instruction and the catalyst for sound, interesting student writing about literary works, I return to Holden's assertions about digression. Despite his chronic inability to explain clearly what he means, Holden unwittingly provides us with a working illustration of digression when he describes a bumbling speech given by his fellow student, Richard Kinsella:

[The students] kept yelling "Digression" at [Richard] the whole time he was making [the speech], and this teacher, Mr. Vinson, gave him an F on it because he hadn't told what kind of animals and vegetables and stuff grew on the farm and all. What he did was, Richard Kinsella, he'd start telling you all about that stuff—then all of a sudden he'd start telling you about this letter his mother got from his uncle, and how his uncle got polio and all when he was forty-two years old, and how he wouldn't let anybody come to see him in the hospital because he didn't want anybody to see him with a brace on. It didn't have much to do with the farm—I admit it—but it was *nice*. It's nice when somebody tells you about their uncle. Especially when they start out telling you about their father's farm and then all of a sudden get more interested in their uncle (Salinger, 183-184).

How often do we make it possible for students to get "nice and excited" over what they read, speak, and write? How often do we instead demand more *evidence* about "the farm" and denounce the digression about "the uncle" as *off the subject*? What is Richard Kinsella's real subject and how did he discover it?

Writing as a mode of discovery is presently a buzz phrase among many teachers who are taking their cue from professional writers.[4] Class discussions (a form of "prewriting") are appropriate and useful occasions for modeling this often elusive notion of discovery. To state the terms of this endeavor rather simply, when discussion—or writing—is truly an act of discovery for a student (and not merely a recycling of someone else's ideas), then as teachers we cannot fault a student such as Richard Kinsella for digressing. Indeed, we should acknowledge what he says and listen carefully so as to encourage him: in the course of his digression he discovers his real subject. From age four we all know that animals live on farms, but we may never know the thoughts of a 42-year-old man suddenly crippled with polio unless someone such as Richard finds a way to articulate that painful experience. Even more essential, I think, is that Richard may never know what he knows, may never understand that experience, unless he is able to give shape and meaning to it through language.

The mode of discovery to which I refer is a process of reconnaissance and investigation that leads to some revelation for the student engaged in that endeavor. In a very serious sense, I lead my students on their own exploration of literature so they can realize for themselves the joy of discovering what they can know. By way of discussion, I want them to get "nice and excited," to get genuinely interested, in what they read and write. When I am successful (which is not always), students teach themselves the discipline of careful observation. Sometimes they unify and simplify what they have observed as one appropriate way of displaying that knowledge. More often, however, they reveal what they have learned through a discursive process of thinking out loud, that is, by talking out their evolving understanding of an idea. When a student engages in this second form of self- expression during a class discussion, both the teacher and other students can actually observe and learn from the student's process of discovering what he or she is coming to learn.[5]

As a teacher I am always principally interested in what students come to think about the literature they read and why. Therefore, I see my role in the classroom (and as a respondent to student writing) as essentially a Socratic one of orchestrating situations in which students can learn from what they read by beginning with what they already know as observant young adults. This approach invests students with the opportunity and responsibility to read carefully and with discrimination, and to write honest, intelligent responses to literature. By creating regular occasions for intensive class discussion, a teacher also provides a formal opportunity for students to talk seriously and purposefully with one another about literature.

To suggest how the practical application of digression works in my classes, I will briefly recount some moments from one class discussion. I recently taught a lower division course in Twentieth Century American Fiction in which we read *The Catcher in the Rye.* Students in this particular class were pursuing many different majors; only two of the thirty-five were English majors. I focus here on *Catcher* because it is familiar to most high school and college English teachers as a text students respond to with confidence and enthusiasm. One of the passages in the novel I wanted students to speculate about was Holden's comment on digression.

I began the day's discussion by asking students to compare the virtues of lecturing with the virtues of discussion. Having spent hundreds of hours in classes, students are experts on effective teaching pedagogies, and most find they have something to say on this subject. On this particular day my students agreed they had had more experience with the lecture format and therefore felt more "comfortable" with it; however, they "got more involved" in a subject when there was a class discussion about it. Once the students had established themselves as authorities on this matter, I turned to *Catcher* and read the passage cited above in which Holden praises digression. I then proposed that Holden's opinion was just one more example of his misplaced sensitivity (an aspect of his character we had already debated at length). I suggested that "it was not the business of educators such as Mr. Vinson or myself to indulge young people such as Holden and my students in youthful, unlettered sentimentalism. Had Mr. Vinson tolerated digression in his students' speeches, he would have been sanctioning intellectual sloppiness—a shameful neglect of his subject and his professional responsibility to discipline the minds of young adults."

As is usually the case when I assume this professional tone and play the devil's advocate (something I do frequently), most students quickly agree with what I proclaim simply because it is obviously the "right" position. In this instance, Mr. Vinson supports the traditional model for student-teacher interaction—the hierarchical model of instruction with which students are most familiar. As professor, my job is to provide students with educated, "right" readings of literature; as model students they, in turn, will recycle the information I provide. If, on the other hand, I have established an atmosphere conducive to dialogue in earlier classes, if I have started off the class with a pertinent passage from the text, and if my comment about that passage gives students room to have their own opinions, then one or two or three students will shake their heads, frown, or shift in their seats, indicating their disagreement with me. Every class discussion—indeed, the entire course —is designed around students' motions of disagreement either with something I or another student has said.

Once a student learns to challenge my position, to assume and defend a different position—in this instance, that digression *is* "nice" and that learning *is* best when a student can get "excited" —then class dialogue is launched for the day. Usually (but again not always), an honest, informed, interesting, and often even passionate exchange of ideas ensues. In this particular class, we moved from talking about Holden's insightful comments on his speech teacher, Mr. Vinson, to his paranoid response to his English teacher, "old Spencer." Along the way, students continually tested their experience against Holden's, which meant discussion frequently wandered far from the novel as students worked out what they sensed, felt, thought, knew, and wondered about the issue under scrutiny.

Because of his embarrassingly adolescent confessions and actions, Holden is a character with whom most students ultimately sympathize, even when they regard him as hopelessly immature. He is good, they reason, because he is sensitive, supersensitive, in a world where most people are phony and don't give a damn. In the class discussion I am describing, students talked at length about the insights into "life" which they shared with Holden. At this point I stopped their digressions and turned back to the novel as a means of testing their understanding of what they had read against what Salinger actually wrote.

I read two passages from *Catcher*. The first is Phoebe and Holden's exchange about the "Catcher in the Rye" song and Robert Burn's poem, when Holden reveals his aspiration to be a catcher. As you will remember, Phoebe points to the critical error in Holden's version of the song: she says the correct lyrics are "If a body *meet* [not *catch*] a body comin' through the rye" (Salinger, 173). Several students expressed their respect for Holden's ambition "to catch everybody if they start to go over the cliff" and cited this as proof of his benevolent nature. No one criticized him. I then turned to the end of the novel and read Holden's thoughts as he watches Phoebe ride the carousel:

Then the carousel started, and I watched her go around and around. There were only about five or six other kids on the ride. . . . All the kids kept trying to grab for the gold ring, and so was old Phoebe, and I was

sort of afraid she'd fall off the goddamn horse, but I didn't say anything or do anything. The thing with kids is, if they want to grab for
the gold ring, you have to let them do it, and not say anything. If they
fall off, they fall off, but it's bad if you say anything to them (Salinger,
211).

Students have seldom read closely enough to see the relationship between these two passages; and if they have, they
strongly resist the implications of the second passage because
it undercuts everything they want to *feel* about Holden. I left
the students with this ambiguity and hoped that with time to
reread and rethink their positions (and with more experience),
they would come to understand what Holden has actually
learned about the dangers of being supersensitive and about
the importance in life of meeting rather than catching people,
especially children.

One student in this class (a senior biology major on his way
to medical school) was a devoted and fierce Salinger fan. He
knew *Catcher* and Holden well, and he loved them. At the
close of our discussion of the novel, he frowningly assured me
that "Holden's view of life and people *was* basically right" and
that he felt "*very* much like Holden about most things." This
student was not alone; other students expressed their sympa-
thy for Holden. I left it at that. But the Salinger fan was not
finished with this novel, as he revealed two months later when
he wrote his final examination (none of which concerned
Catcher). On the last page of his blue book, after he had answered the exam questions, he wrote the following comment
which I regard as a consequence of our having pursued digression as a mode of discovery throughout the entire course:

I've been thinking about this ever since I last read *The Catcher in
the Rye*. What is the definition of a good book? How about this? Being
able to see something (a meaning) different every time one reads it.

That's why *Catcher* is so good. The last time I read it, it took on a
completely different meaning than before. Before it was a view of the
world through somebody who could really see the truth. Now the
meaning is different. And it is very difficult to discuss. But it has to do
with being so depressed that everything in the world looks like crap

(phony, etc.). This ("phony") is not true. Sally Hayes and Stradlater were, as I see them now, your typical fun-loving kids. Holden was so damn depressed about his life. Really. He was searching for something to love. He told Sally he loved her. He didn't. But he wanted to love something. Even that "goddamn Maurice." Anyway—

Notes

1. In the accompanying list of works cited, I have included the early books by these authors, as well as subsequent works by them. All five are still actively engaged in writing about writing.

2. For information about regional writing projects affiliated with The National Writing Project (there are more than 100 project sites nation-wide), write to The National Writing Project, 5635 Tolman Hall, School of Education, University of California, Berkeley, CA 94720.

3. Murray (*Write to Learn*, 6-9) provides a useful introductory discussion and illustration of the process model, and in *Learning by Teaching* (3-96) he discusses in depth many relevant issues. Two helpful discussions of the reading process are Bruce Petersen's "In Search of Meaning: Readers and Expressive Language," and Thomas Newkirk's "Looking for Trouble: A Way to Unmask our Readings."

4. See Janet Emig's "Writing as a Mode of Learning" for a theoretical discussion; and Lil Brannon (76-102) and Don Murray (*Write to Learn*, passim) for practical applications.

5. A useful presentation of this discovery process as revealed in student writing is provided by Thomas Newkirk. See also William Zeiger, "The Exploratory Essay: Enfranchising the Spirit of Inquiry in College Composition."

Works Cited

Berthoff, Ann E. *The Making of Meaning: Metaphors, Models, and Maxims for Writing Teachers.* Montclair, NJ: Boynton/Cook Publishers, 1981.

Brannon, Lil, Melinda Knight, Vara Neverow-Turk. *Writers Writing.* Montclair, NJ: Boynton/Cook Publishers, 1982.

Coles, William E., Jr. *The Plural I: The Teaching of Writing.* New York: Holt, Rinehart and Winston, 1973.

Elbow, Peter. *Writing with Power.* New York: Oxford University Press, 1981.

———. *Writing Without Teachers.* New York: Oxford University Press, 1983.

Emig, Janet. "Writing as a Mode of Learning." *College Composition and Communication* 28 (May 1977): 122-127.

Fulwiler, Toby. "The Personal Connection: Journal Writing Across the Curriculum." *Language Connections: Writing and Reading Across the Curriculum.* Eds. Toby Fulwiler and Art Young. Urbana, IL: National Council of Teachers of English, 1982. 15-31.

Healy, Mary K. "Using Student Writing Response Groups." *Theory and Practice in the Teaching of Composition.* Eds. Miles Myers and James Gray. Urbana, IL: National Council of Teachers of English, 1983. 159-162.

Kirby, Dan and Tom Liner. *Inside Out: Developmental Strategies for Teaching Writing.* Montclair, NJ: Boynton/Cook Publishers, 1981.

Koch, Carl and James M. Brazil. *Strategies for Teaching the Composition Process.* Urbana, IL: National Council of Teachers of English, 1978.

Macrorie, Ken. *Searching Writing: A Contextbook.* Montclair, NJ: Boynton/Cook Publishers, 1984.

———. *Telling Writing.* Hayden Writing Series. Montclair, NJ: Boynton/Cook Publishers, 3rd ed., 1980.

Moffett, James. *Active Voice: A Writing Program Across the Curriculum.* Montclair, NJ: Boynton/Cook Publishers, 1981.

———. *Teaching the Universe of Discourse.* New York: Houghton Mifflin, 1968.

Murray, Donald. *Learning by Teaching: Selected Articles on Writing and Teaching.* Montclair, NJ: Boynton/Cook Publishers, 1982.

———. *Write to Learn.* New York: Holt, Rinehart and Winston, 1984.

Newkirk, Thomas. "Looking for Trouble: A Way to Unmask Our Readings. *College English* 26 (December 1984): 756-766.

Petersen, Bruce. "In Search of Meaning: Readers and Expressive Language." *Language Connections: Writing and Reading across the Curriculum.* Eds. Toby Fulwiler and Art Young. Urbana, IL: National Council of Teachers of English, 1982. 107-122.

Rico, Gabriele Lusser. *Balancing the Hemispheres: Brain Research and the Teaching of Writing.* Bay Area Writing Project Monograph. Berkeley, CA: University of California, 1980.

———. *Writing the Natural Way.* Los Angeles: Tarcher, Inc., 1983.

Rosenblatt, Louise M. *The Reader, the Text, the Poem: The Transanctional Theory of the Literary Work.* Carbondale, IL: Southern Illinois University Press, 1978.

Salinger, J. D. *The Catcher in the Rye.* New York: Bantam Books, 1951.

Winterowd, W. Ross. *The Contemporary Writer.* New York: Harcourt Brace, 1981.

Zeiger, William. "The Exploratory Essay: Enfranchising the Spirit of Inquiry in College Composition." *College English* 47 (September 1985): 454-466.

Subject Matter and Gender

Ann Lavine

> Silence can be a plan
> rigorously executed
>
> the blueprint to a life
>
> It is a presence
> it has a history   a form
>
> Do not confuse it
> with any kind of absence
>
> >   Adrienne Rich
> >   "Cartographies of Silence" (16-20)

At our last departmental grading session we discussed three papers about romantic experiences. The students had been asked to analyze a successful or unsuccessful romantic experience in terms of either its causes or effects. Most of the faculty present agreed that all three papers were in the C to D range according to the grading standards generated by the department. But although the final determinations were similar, the reasons for them were not. The two male writers related details copiously but analyzed their experience only sparingly. ("I took a forty-minute shower and for the first time, shaved my entire face, not leaving a hair to be seen." "I was supposed to pick up my date, Sue, at 8:00, but I lost track of time and didn't pull into her driveway until about 8:35.") Their use of narration without analysis, coupled with numerous surface errors, were the primary reasons given for the C to D grades.

The female writer, on the other hand, composed an almost perfect paper in terms of organization and mechanics but wrote mostly in generalities, giving only a superficial account of a specific incident. People even questioned whether or not the experience referred to was real, so vacuous were the details. ("An equally shared conversation is a first requirement for good communication. . . .On my date, Scott and I were able to talk and listen for equal amounts of time, which allowed us to feel comfortable.")

While these three papers hardly constitute a representative sampling of male and female writing, they do raise some interesting questions about the ways women and men approach subject matter. For example, why did the female writer when required by the nature of the assignment to write about an experience *as a female*, hide behind platitudes without delving into any kind of meaningful specifics? Since her paper was textbook perfect in almost every other aspect, one assumes there was some kind of choice on her part. As Mina Shaughnessy explains so well in *Errors and Expectations*, students seldom make random mistakes, rather, they make decisions based on beliefs they hold, however spurious (5). What belief then did this woman, a good student, hold that caused her, when asked to analyze an experience as a female, to skillfully and artfully avoid doing just that? Conversely, what beliefs did the male writers hold that caused them to happily provide an abundance of details, many embarrassingly confessional? ("I had a perfect evening planned, first the arcade, then off to a movie, out for a snack, and then after that whatever came natural between a man and a woman." "She stood about five feet, six inches tall and weighted [sic] about 110 pound. I remember every shape and contour of her body with great fondness.")

An obvious explanation for their different approaches can be found in the different receptions usually accorded writings which reflect female experiences and those which reflect male experiences. Traditionally, writing by women, regardless of subject matter, has not been well received, but writing by women using distinctly female experiences as subject matter has been even less well received. As Virginia Woolf in *A Room of One's Own* observes, "This is an important book, the critic assumes, because it deals with war. This is an insignificant book because it deals with the feelings of women in a drawing-room" (77).[1] A less obvious explanation of the female writer's decision to avoid the subject matter may be found in the recent research on the patterns of conversational interactions used by women and men. An examination of this research will be helpful in understanding this student's decision.

Clearly there are limitations in using research on verbal behavior to more fully explain writing behavior, and they mainly result from the differences between speech and writing. Although many of the features of speech and writing are similar, the two are not altogether isomorphic, and it would be simplistic to treat them so. What holds true for one cannot automatically be assumed to hold true for the other. The value of such an approach, however, is that both speech and writing are discourse acts; namely, they consist of the interactions among speaker/writer, listener/reader, and message/text. In each case, someone is communicating something to someone else, and it is the ability of the speaker/writer to balance the three elements which determine the success or failure of a particular discourse. With regard to the student writers, knowledge of their conversational patterns, while it will not fully account for their writing choices, will certainly shed some light on them.

Conversational patterns which best illuminate the students' choices are those which operate to control the direction and content of conversations. Examples of such patterns can be found in the research of Candace West and Don Zimmerman (1975, 1983). For their first study, West and Zimmerman examined two-party conversations between acquaintances and compared the use of interruptions and overlaps in same-sex conversations with their use in cross sex-conversations. They defined interruptions as "violations" of conversational turn-taking (for example, speaking in the middle of someone's utterance). Overlaps were "errors" in turn-taking (for example, miscalculating the end of a person's utterance and speaking simultaneously with their last word). They considered expressions such as *mmhmm, uh huh,* and *yeah* supportive utterances, not interruptions or overlaps. Although West and Zimmerman found equal numbers of interruptions and overlaps in same sex conversations, in cross sex conversations they found that males made ninety-six percent of the interruptions and one hundred percent of the overlaps.

In addition to making more active infractions in conversational turn-taking, the men in their study made more passive ones as well. For example, they often paused anywhere from three to ten seconds before providing a supportive utterance for their female partners. As with interruptions and overlaps, these pauses were not present in the same sex conversations. West and Zimmerman discovered that the use of all three infractions combined to operate in much the same way: namely, after a certain number, the topic under discussion was dropped.

West and Zimmerman's initial study was criticized for examining conversations between acquaintances, because it was thought that friends would take more liberties when communicating, and hence, the infractions could not be considered as gregarious as they appeared. So West and Zimmerman repeated their study using unacquainted persons (1983). While the percentages were lower for this study, the men still made seventy-five percent of the interruptions, three times more than the women. In addition, West and Zimmerman found that when women did interrupt, they interrupted much later in the men's utterances than the men interrupted in the women's.

Differences in male and female conversational patterns were also discovered in a recent study by Pamela Fishman (1983). After examining the household conversations of three heterosexual couples, Fishman found that the women did much more of the conversational "work" than the men. For example, the women asked two and one-half times the questions the men asked; they also consistently provided supportive utterances, timed so that they rarely overlapped the men's statements. But despite the conversational "work" being performed by the women, Fishman found that the men clearly controlled the choice of topics. Of the twenty-nine topics raised by men, twenty-eight were successfully pursued, but of the forty-seven raised by the women, only seventeen were pursued. The thirty topics which failed did so because of a lack of response on the part of the men. Fishman concludes, "The definition of what is appropriate or inappropriate conversation becomes the man's choice" (98).

Although the ways in which women and men verbally interact are just beginning to be studied and much more research is needed, including studies on the influence of other factors such as class and race, the evidence amassed so far in this area clearly points to certain conclusions. First of all, it seems that gender differences in conversational patterns exist; men and women may theoretically have access to all patterns and no doubt use them all at some time or another, but in reality, women use certain patterns significantly more often than men and vice versa. Secondly, the use of these patterns reflects and maintains the lower status of women in our society. Francine Frank and Frank Anshen observe in *Language and the Sexes* that "conversations . . . seem to represent in microcosm the distribution of power in other areas of our lives" (33). West and Zimmerman write, "It . . . appears that whenever males and females talk, there are discernible echoes of 'a sexual division of labor'" ("Small Insults," 110).

Turning back to our original concern, we need now to ask what these findings on verbal behavior can tell us about the writing behavior of our three students. James Moffett argues that in order to be successful "a writer of whatever age has to feel full of herself [sic] and have a degree of confidence, belief that she has something to say, faith in her will, and control of her attention" (70). Indeed, it seems all too obvious that writers must have confidence in themselves, their audience, and their subject matter. Yet as writing teachers, we often assume our students either have this attitude of confidence or have not really applied themselves yet. But what attitudes must our female and male students hold about their identities as writers, their use of their reality as legitimate subject matter, or their audience's willingness to listen, when one gender's thoughts are interrupted and the other gender's elicited and encouraged? When one gender's topics are ignored and the other's usually taken up and discussed? When it comes to the task of sitting down and writing—as with conversing—women seem to be at a distinct disadvantage.

This handicap does not mean, however, that women do not produce good writing. As Johanna Drucker explains in an article on women and writing, "The question of whether women can or will use language with authority is a moot point. We do" (57). The real question concerns the compensations and compromises women must make in order to have their writing well received. In the area of subject matter, it seems the compromise is to avoid writing about topics which point out the femaleness of the author unless she decides to risk disapproval or dismissal as someone who has something significant to say. And given the usual reception of women's topics in verbal behavior, disapproval or dismissal is almost a certainty. The female writer's behavior now seems not only understandable, but reasonable. As Virginia Woolf notes, "It is fatal for a woman to lay the least stress on any grievance; to plead even with justice any cause; in any way to speak consciously as a woman" (108).

The solutions to this problem do not lie in avoiding certain subject matters in our writing assignments, nor do they lie exclusively within the walls of the classroom, since the problem clearly does not. However, understanding why students make certain choices, along with gently encouraging them to grapple with and reflect their unique realities in their writings, will go a long way in producing better writers. Moffett writes, "What really teaches composition—'putting together'—is disorder. Clarity and objectivity become learning challenges only when content and form are *not* given to the learner but when she [sic] must find and forge her own from her inchoate thought" (67).

In summary, then, I would like to suggest a few measures we can take as writing teachers to help our female students. To begin with, we can broaden our own notions of appropriate subject matter and communicate that to our students. Sheila Ortiz Taylor in an article on women and writing reminds us that "the term *essay* . . . as coined by Montaigne, was intended to emphasize the free nature of the form" (387). In keeping with that definition, we can encourage (not require) students to take risks and tackle non- traditional subject matter.

Another suggestion involves providing activities which help the students focus on themselves as writers. Joan Bolker hypothesizes in "Teaching Griselda to Write" that the reason two of her best female students describe "a lack of personality" and a "sense of non-ownership" in their papers is because they place undue emphasis on deference to their audience at the expense of asserting themselves as writers (906). Bolker explains that when a person writes only to please her audience and never herself, "ambivalence is out, changes of mind are out, the important nagging questions are out, because they are not neat, and they might offend" (907). One way of helping students to focus on themselves as writers is to have them examine their own writing pasts, perhaps providing them with a model of such an examination as Tillie Olsen's "Silences." Have them focus on the kinds of writing they have done (both inside the classroom and out), the subject matters they have used, and the reactions they have received.[2]

And last, and perhaps most important, we need to listen to our students and be the kind of critical, yet generous audience they need. As Adrienne Rich says, we need to

[l]isten to a woman groping for language in which to express what is on her mind, sensing that the terms of academic discourse are not her language, trying to cut down her thought to the dimensions of a discourse not intended for her (for it is not fitting that a woman speak in public); or reading her paper aloud at breakneck speed, throwing her words away, deprecating her own work by a reflex prejudgment: I do not deserve to take up time and space ("Taking," 243-244).

Or, I might add, writing a paper about a romantic experience in which there is no evidence of an author behind the words. Only by listening to and encouraging that voice will we be able to really teach our female students to write truthfully and write well.

Notes

1. For an excellent collection of remarks by critics about women's writing see Johanna Russ, *How to Suppress*

Women's Writing (Austin, TX: University of Texas Press, 1983).

    2. Additionally, the importance of using prewriting and invention heuristics seems self-evident. Students must be given not only the tools but the time to explore their ideas and the implications of those ideas before turning them into readable prose.

Works Cited

Bolker, Joan. "Teaching Griselda to Write." *College English* 40 (April, 1979): 906-908.

Drucker, Johanna. "Women and Language." *Poetics Journal* 4 (May 1984): 56-68.

Fishman, Pamela M. "Interaction: The Work Women Do." *Language, Gender and Society.* Eds. Barrie Thorne, Cheris Kramarae and Nancy Henley. Rowley, MA: Newbury House Publishers, Inc., 1983. 89-101.

Frank, Francine, and Frank Anshen. *Language and the Sexes.* Albany, NY: State University of New York Press, 1983.

Moffett, James. "Writing, Inner Speech, and Meditation." *Rhetoric and Composition.* Upper Montclair, NJ: Boynton/Cook Publishers, Inc., 1984. 65-80.

Olsen, Tillie. "Silences in Literature - 1962." *Silences.* New York: Delacorte Press/Seymour Lawrence, 1978. 5-21.

Rich, Adrienne. "Cartographies of Silence." *The Dream of a Common Language: Poems 1974-1977.* New York: W. W. Norton and Company, Inc., 1978. 16-20.

———. "Taking Women Students Seriously." *On Lies, Secrets, and Silence: Selected Prose 1966-1978.* New York: W. W. Norton and Company, 1979. 237-245.

Shaughnessy, Mina P. *Errors and Expectations: A Guide for the Teacher of Basic Writing.* New York: Oxford University Press, 1977.

Taylor, Sheila Ortiz. "Women in a Double-Bind: Hazards of the Argumentative Edge." *College Composition and Communications* 29 (December, 1978): 385-389.

West, Candace, and Don H. Zimmerman. "Sex Roles, Interruption and Silences in Conversation." *Language and Sex: Difference and Dominance.* Eds. Barrie Thorne and Nancy Henley. Rowley, MA: Newbury House Publishers, Inc., 1975. 105-129.

———. "Small Insults: A Study of Interruptions in Cross-Sex Conversations between Unacquainted Persons." *Language, Gender and Society.* Eds. Barrie Thorne, Cheris Kramarae and Nancy Henley. Rowley, MA: Newbury House Publishers, Inc., 1983. 102-117.

Woolf, Virginia. *A Room of One's Own.* 1929. Rpt. New York: Harcourt, Brace, and World, Inc., 1957.

Chapter Four

Equity In Practice

This chapter offers examples of equity in practice in the classroom. The essays address such topics as encouraging students to participate in the power of language and making journal writing a significant part of the course. They also offer helpful models of course formats and assignments. The authors provide descriptions of their rationales and methodologies, and an evaluation of success.

Valuing Language: Feminist Pedagogy in the Writing Classroom

Pattie Cowell

I. Rationale

After twelve years of experience as a writing teacher, in contexts ranging from high school "remedial" to "advanced" undergraduate courses, I have concluded that the fundamental problems facing apprentice writers (regardless of basic skill levels) are the same. Whether the writers are high school "discipline problems" or pre-law students at prestigious universities, they distrust words and themselves. They view language as a mystical system linking people and ideas in inherently unknowable ways. Their understanding of how language functions approaches superstition. What we sometimes label "carelessness" with language is the direct result of a distrust of language as a bearer of meanings, of a sense that exact language doesn't really matter. Worried about "correctness" rather than "effectiveness" in their writing, students search for a formula, for "what-the-teacher-wants" (Bunch, 259).

Whatever the reasons apprentice writers have come to distrust language and their ability to use it, a writing classroom shaped by feminist pedagogy will address these issues directly.

II. Methodology

What easier way to explore the "magic" of connotation than by examining what Muriel Schulz has termed "the semantic derogation of women" (64). Compare the connotations of "bachelor" and "spinster," of "master" and "mistress," of

"courtier" and "courtesan." If those distinctions are too obvious, trace the history of changing definitions for a term such as
"harlot," which originally referred to persons of either sex and
was used to describe men more often than women. Or discuss
the implications of labels such as "pro-choice" and "pro-abor-
tion" for groups supporting women's rights to reproductive
freedom. Class members usually supplement such examples
with suggestions of their own, and with new questions. What
do changing connotations imply about our cultures? Can we
use language toward a re-vision of our cultures, of ourselves?
Once the reciprocal relationship between language and culture
is clear, the applications are infinite. Distinctions between
"master" and "mistress" are not, after all, so different in kind
from the distinctions between "illegal aliens" and "undocu-
mented workers," or between "technical discomfort" and a
"nuclear accident." Apprentice writers may find that they
need not be awed by the "magic" of such language: they can
both use it and avoid being used by it.

Such "magic" attaches itself to more than word choice. A
writer's assumptions, those conscious or unconscious preconceptions which shape our worlds and our writing, are seldom
directly articulated. Uncritical readers miss the ideas and values beneath the surface of an essay, their own or someone
else's. For that reason, I often preface writing instruction with
practice in critical reading. Bringing several examples of advertising into the classroom, I ask class members to identify the
tacit assumptions behind an ad's appeal. What can they infer
about sex role assumptions from a Clairol ad which pictures a
well-dressed woman saying "On men, gray hair is distin-
guished. On me, it's just plain old." Or from a Seagram's ad
which pictures a broken bottle of whiskey with the caption
"Have you ever seen a grown man cry?" I may even ask class
members to unravel the assumptions behind a male student's
opening assertion for a class assignment: "Every man is different in his or her own way."

Such examples provide obvious sparks for discussion, of
course, but the process of identifying both the surface argument *and its implications* transfers easily into the analysis of
more complicated materials. More of the magical power of lan-

guage is within students' grasp: if they can identify the assumptions behind the arguments of others, they can identify their own (Bunch, 255).

III. Evaluation

Feminist instruction encourages writers to replace their distrust of language with an active participation in its power. Class discussions of the connotative effect of words reveal an almost magical force in language, but not of the supernatural variety. Writers discover that "mere matters of words" have an enormous impact on the minds of those who use them and those who hear them. I have been suggesting a variety of classroom activities which may replace writers' distrust of language with the analytical skills to use their language effectively. Many of the lessons are difficult ones, not only because learning new skills is always difficult but also because unlearning old myths is painful. Once writers accept a contextual framework for their work, they must accept a number of corollaries as well—that language can create and recreate boundaries to perception, that the product of writing is intimately related to the process from which it comes, that complete objectivity as a writer (or as a reader) is impossible. Some approach these concepts with ambivalence, others as a clarification of "what-I've-known-all-along." But whatever the response, as writing is perceived in relation to human experience, apprentice writers recognize the value—both senses intended—of their own voices.

Works Cited

Bunch, Charlotte. "Not By Degrees: Feminist Theory and Education." *Learning Our Way: Essays in Feminist Education.* Eds. Charlotte Bunch and Sandra Pollack. Trumansburg, NY: The Crossing Press, 1983. 248-260.

Schulz, Muriel R. "The Semantic Derogation of Woman." *Language and Sex: Difference and Dominance.* Eds. Barrie Thorne and Nancy Henley. Rowley, MA: Newbury House, 1975. 64-75.

Making Journal Writing Matter

Donna M. Perry

I. Rationale

I have assigned journals in my classes for about seven years and have used them in various ways: to help students record impressions, work through problems, practice skills we have demonstrated and discussed in class, or explore ideas for possible papers.[1] But the assignment has always had mixed results, with many students claiming that they found the regular writing tedious, that they didn't know what to write about (even after I had given them dozens of suggested topics), that they did not find it relevant to the other writing done in the course or to their own lives. Until recently, my rationale was that such writing was doing them some good that they didn't realize. I used a sports metaphor to make my point: writing is like playing tennis. You must practice that forehand return off a backboard many times before you can go up against an opponent and play competitively. Journal writing was a kind of practice for the real thing.

Now I have changed my motives and my metaphor: I assign journal writing for its subversive elements and I see it as more like underwater exploring than like competitive sports. My writing classes are examining things that matter—issues of injustices that float under the surface calm of their own lives—and speaking to me in radically new ways. The journal assignment now accomplishes two things beyond merely practice in writing: it subverts the structured, hierarchical relationship between my students and me and it provides my students with a "safe place" in which to critically examine their worlds.

I reconceptualized student journal writing after I assigned it in "Women's Changing Roles," a required, introductory-level women's studies course which I started teaching last year. Here I was not trying to improve my students' writing; I was just hoping that with a little encouragement they would connect what they were learning with what they were living. To my surprise, the assignment did this and more. There were at least three direct results: most students enjoyed journal writing and did so regularly throughout the course; the traditional student-teacher relationship broke down in the journals as we spoke to one another in a more personal way; and the journal writing itself gave my students a place in which to write about what for them were taboo subjects (homosexuality, abortion, etc.).[2]

II. Methodology

On the syllabus for "Women's Changing Roles," I had given this description of the journal assignment:

As part of your course requirements, I ask that you keep a journal in which to record responses to the readings, classes, outside readings you do on your own, or experiences that you have. This should be an 8-½ by 11" notebook with detachable pages so that samples can be handed in when requested. I ask that you write AT LEAST three pages per week, but you can write more if you wish. While I will recommend topics as the course progresses, you should feel free to address those questions that concern you in this journal, for you are, ultimately, the audience for it. This journal should be a place in which you ask questions and move toward answers—it should provide you with a quiet, safe place in which to grapple with some of the thorny issues we will be dealing with in the coming weeks. You will hand in the journal for evaluation, but at that time you can staple, clip, or otherwise limit my access to individual sections by closing them off. I will be checking the six pages you indicate with a check as representing your best work. Occasionally, I may ask you to hand in some pages or to write, so BRING THE JOURNAL TO CLASS WITH YOU.

To further stress the non-punitive nature of the journal assignment, I made it count for only 1/6th of the course grade and
assured them that they would get an A for just handing in the
required 48 pages. Early in the semester I collected some journal pages and read a few interesting ones to the class to show
them the variety of responses possible. To help them see the
journal as a place to make connections, I often asked them to
write in class in response to guest speakers, films, or class
discussion.

The success of the journals in my women's studies classes
prompted me to wonder what I had been doing wrong in composition. Admittedly, many of the women's studies students
were older (this was an evening class) and most (90%) were
women, but this was still a required course with mostly first-
year students and sophomores. So why the difference?

I became convinced that journal writing becomes a valuable
learning activity for students when a) it is seen (by teacher and
students) as an integral part of the course; b) its relation to
other aspects of the course is clear; and c) it serves as a "safe
place" where students can explore the implications for their
own lives of ideas raised in the course. The journals worked so
well in my women's studies course because students (at least
the women) found them relevant. If I could make the activity
similarly relevant in writing classes, it might work.

Since one problem with my old "list of possible journal topics" approach was that students weren't really engaged in writing about these artificial assignments, I resolved to design
questions that would get them thinking about their lives. My
writing assignments moved students from the personal to the
public world, so I could fashion journal assignments around
this general topic: the different worlds we inhabit and the roles
we play.[3]

I gave my composition classes a description of the journal assignment that was similar to that for women's studies, in
terms of format, number of entries, etc. (see above). But I added
this section for focus:

This semester you will be asked to think about the roles you play:
in the private world of home, friends, and family, and the public

worlds of school, work, neighborhood, city, country, world. You will be writing papers about these roles, but I want you to consider them at greater length, and privately, in a journal.

To help you focus on the roles you play, here are some suggested journal topics grouped by weeks. Each week, use your journal to explore at length some of these questions or others that might never find their way into your papers but are still important to you.

Following this, I gave them specific topics which led them to examine their worlds in new ways. For example, during the week when they were writing about a person who had influenced them, I suggested the following writing prompts: "Collect life stories from people around you: the security guard in the dorm, the neighborhood grocer, the waitress in a restaurant you frequent, etc." When they were examining the media, I suggested: "Examine a few of the following and consider whether you share the values they represent or not: soap operas, game shows, commercials, MTV, news programs." During the weeks on an issue paper, I offered these topics: "Is your job sex-stereotyped? Write about that" or "Imagine that you had to change your race or sex. Which would you change? How would your life be different? Why?"

III. Evaluation

I have tried this approach to journal assignments for two semesters now and it seems to be working: at end-of the-semester evaluations, 70% of my students said that they enjoyed keeping the journals. I am sure that the activity is more relevant now—to the papers they are writing and to their lives beyond the classroom. Many are relating to me in a more personal way, saying things in their journal that they wouldn't say in class (a student wrote a page explaining why I didn't understand a poem she has submitted; another expressed shyness about talking in front of the group). In addition, as reader I have a chance to relate to my students not as writing coach or evaluator (the two roles I play most often) but as an interested observer, sometimes a bit of a student myself (as when a student wrote about his hobby of rappelling).

Most important, the journal assignments have provided my students with a way to think about their worlds that may help them to question and change them. As one white male student wrote: "I never really thought about what life would be like if I was [sic] black, but everything would be different." When he went on to consider why this is so, he was forced to recognize the reality of racism, perhaps for the first time.

It is too soon for me to know if the assignment will be as successful with writing classes as it has been with women's studies. But I do know that this use of student journal writing makes more sense than the tennis practice I was demanding before. My students and I have become writers in search of meanings. Like Adrienne Rich's underwater explorer, we dive below the surface reality to discover what lies beneath. Like her, we can say:

> The words are purposes.
> The words are maps.
> I came to see the damage that was done
> And the treasures that prevail.
>   "Diving Into the Wreck," (23).

Notes

1. For the use of journals and writing across the curriculum in general see Toby Fulwiler, "The Personal Connection: Journal Writing Across the Curriculum," pp. 15-31 in Toby Fulwiler and Burt Young, eds. *Language Connections: Reading and Writing Across the Curriculum* (Urbana, IL: National Council of Teachers of English, 1982) or C. H. Knoblauch and Lil Brannon, "Writing as Learning through the Curriculum," *College English* 45 (Sept. 1983): 465-474.

2. I assigned readings from Mary Jane Moffat and Charlotte Painter, eds. *Revelations: Diaries of Women* (New York: Vintage Books, 1974); Lyn Lifshin, ed. *Ariadne's Thread: A Collection of Contemporary Women's Journals* (New York: Harper and Row, 1982); and Cherrie Moraga and Gloria Anzaldùa, eds. *This Bridge Called My Back: Writing by Radical*

Women of Color, 2nd ed. (New York: Kitchen Table: Women of Color Press, 1983) to establish a tradition of women journal writers.

     3. This division of assignments is suggested in the excellent text *Four Worlds of Writing*, eds. Janice M. Lauer, Gene Montague, Andrea Lunsford, and Janet Emig (New York: Harper and Row, 1981).

Works Cited

Rich, Adrienne. "Diving Into the Wreck." *Diving Into the Wreck: Poems 1971-72*. New York: W. W. Norton and Company, Inc., 1973. 22-24.

Becoming Gender Conscious: Writing About Sex Roles in a Composition Course

James D. Riemer

I. Rationale

While my experience with composition classes has shown me that most college first-year students have very definite ideas and attitudes about feminism and gender roles and are usually willing to express them verbally and often quite stridently, many times they fail to recognize the great degree to which socially prescribed ideals of desirable and acceptable masculine and feminine behavior continue to affect and limit their growth as individuals. Thus, when given the opportunity to teach an honors composition class focused on a single theme, I was eager to design a class that would center entirely on discussing and writing about the nature and effects of gender roles in contemporary society.

Because my major objective in teaching the class was to prompt students to question society's rigidly defined gender roles as well as to become aware of the ways in which these roles affect their own lives, the essays and additional readings were selected to give specifically feminist, liberal views on the matter of gender roles. I was certain that, having been exposed to society's predominant attitudes towards strongly differentiated roles and behaviors for men and women for at least seventeen or eighteen years, most students would have familiarity with the opposing traditional and conservative views of sex roles, whereas they were much more unlikely to have given thoughtful consideration to liberal, less traditional attitudes.

II. Methodology

A major concern in designing the course was how to discuss gender roles for a fifteen-week semester without a sense of repetitiousness and *deja vu* setting in shortly after the fourth week. My first precaution was to select two collections of essays (Gornick and Moran's *Woman in Sexist Society*, and Pleck and Sawyer's *Men and Masculinity*) which would indicate the complexity of the subject by allowing the class discussion to focus separately on five or six distinct but related issues concerning sex roles, including such topics as images of men and women in advertising; male and female attitudes toward competition, work, and success; views of male and female sexuality; relationships with the opposite sex; friendships with the same sex; and images of men and women in literature. The ideas raised in these essays would then be applied to Ernest Hemingway's *The Sun Also Rises* and Lisa Alther's *Kinflicks*, a satiric chronicle of a young woman's attempts to find her identity through a series of sexual relationships and by conforming to a gamut of stereotypes of womanhood from cheerleader to intellectual spinster to radical lesbian to suburban housewife.

A second precaution was to avoid any extensive overview discussion of traditional sex roles and their limitations or drawbacks. Therefore, rather than beginning the course with several essays summarizing the major dissatisfactions which feminism and men's liberation have with our society's rigidly defined and applied gender roles, we launched into a discussion of the images of men and women in advertising. This in-depth consideration of one of the most influential and pervasive means by which our society defines and perpetuates sex roles would serve as a foundation for future discussions by permitting students to grasp some of the traditional values and behaviors that our society deems acceptable and desirable for men and women.

Since the major goal of the course was for the individual to examine his or her own life and values in relation to our society's gender roles, an important element of the course work, aside from writing essays, took the form of a semester-long journal in which students wrote personal responses to one or several of the readings assigned for a particular class session. Although I read and wrote comments in the journals, I did so under a promise of confidentiality. The journals were essentially anonymous, identified only by social security number, with records of journal requirements not correlated with students' names until the end of the semester. The private nature of the journals was to encourage personal introspection. The journal provided an opportunity for students to reveal feelings, thoughts, and personal experiences they might have felt uneasy about sharing with the class, particularly if they felt their views went against those expressed in the readings or by other students in class discussions. The journals also gave me an opportunity to stimulate students to look deeper into their own experiences to validate or challenge their views and values as well as those expressed in class readings and discussion.

III. Evaluation

Throughout the fifteen weeks of the course, discussion was almost always lively and thoughtful, although there was an initial not unexpected difficulty and self-consciousness when the discussions focused on sexuality and sexual relationships. End of semester evaluations revealed that the students almost unanimously found the readings and discussion provocative, insightful and relevant. Most students also found the journals valuable for stimulating their thoughts about the readings and for providing material for their own essays.

There are, however, a few changes that I would make if I were to teach the class again. Although the anthology *Women in Sexist Society* was excellent for presenting many of the essential feminist concerns, students frequently felt that some of its essays were outdated. Also, the somewhat complex, scholarly nature of many of the essays suffered in students' eyes when contrasted with the essays in *Men and Masculinity*, which were often more personal, humorous, and ironic. Thus, I would balance or possibly replace the feminist readings in the Gornick and Moran text with more recent essays that would accurately reflect the current state of feminism and society's attitudes toward women, as well as reveal the personal, "hu-

man," often humorous side of feminist writing. I would also replace the Hemingway novel, which students had difficulty
relating to their own lives, with another novel that deals with
images and ideals of manhood more closely connected to their
experiences and goals, for instance, Lewis' *Babbitt* or Farrel's
Young Manhood of Studs Lonigan.

While I have focused here on the course as an exchange of
ideas and an examination of the nature and effects of gender
roles, I want to stress that the class was also remarkably successful as a course on composition because of its subject matter. Students were engaged in writing about an issue which
they found strikingly relevant to their own lives and for which
they had a vast storehouse of personal experience to be re-ex-
amined in a new light. Because this relevancy and new perspective were intertwined, for these students, writing became a
process of discovery about self and society.

Writing About Families: How to Apply Feminism to a Traditional Writing Syllabus

Susan Radner

I. Rationale

At William Paterson College, a New Jersey state college, the syllabus for Writing Effective Prose, a three-credit composition class required of all students, is very restrictive. It emphasizes the different rhetorical types—description, narration, definition, explanation of a process, comparison and contrast, argumentation, research. Instructors must assign a minimum number (five) of five-hundred-word papers. Students must revise each paper after a conference with the instructor. Instructors must use a handbook-rhetoric, which we choose from a small list; a book of readings is optional. Absolutely forbidden is the teaching of literature, which is somehow seen as irrelevant both to the needs of our students (mainly business majors) and to the teaching of writing itself. We must give letter grades, and students must achieve a *C* to pass the course. This syllabus has not changed very much in the twenty or so years I have been teaching the course.

I have changed, however. Teaching in the women's studies program and working in a more egalitarian setting with women students has made me more sensitive to the problems and fears of all students, fears which they may be reluctant to reveal. Therefore, I try to create a supportive atmosphere in my classroom. I hold conferences with all students where we discuss the problems the students had in writing their essays. I give students a checklist of what to look for in each paper and then have them work in groups of three or four revising their essays. I "count" the revision of their papers more than their first drafts, and I give flexible deadlines. Borrowing from my women's studies classes, I ask composition students to keep personal journals in which they write three times a week. While women students find this easier to do than men at first because they kept diaries when they were younger, eventually even the men catch on and they begin to feel more comfortable expressing their feelings on paper.

As feminist English teachers, we bring our feminism into every class we teach. However, since we often are confronted with the kinds of rigid course syllabi I have described and "non-political" or hostile colleagues, this infusion of a feminist perspective may be difficult. I have found a way to fulfill the requirements of a standard syllabus for a first-year student writing course and at the same time infuse it with feminist content. I do this by organizing all the writing topics and class discussions around the theme of the contemporary family.

II. Methodology

One technique (transposed from my women's studies classes) is simply to use details from women's lives to illustrate various points I wish to make. For example, in teaching how to make lists in order to organize an outline, I ask students how they make up their grocery shopping lists, and lead them to see that they group items according to some organizing principle, usually location in the store. In teaching spatial order, I ask them to describe their kitchens. For a process exercise, I ask them how to cook a meal, or how to clean a room. These exercises give positive reinforcement to the older women students, who see these chores as "their" work. But by giving the exercises at the same time to men to do, I suggest that men are and should be doing the work too. Then after the exercise is over, we discuss how the roles of men and women are changing today.

The most radical change I have made is in the structuring of topics for class discussion and student papers. Instead of using a book of essays on general topics, as we are encouraged to do, I have eliminated a reader altogether.

I focus on the theme of the family and the community and integrate these ideas into my teaching of the different rhetorical types which I have to "cover" according to our syllabus. Some of my specific assignments are:

1. For *description*: "Describe your community (street, neighborhood, town) and say why you live there or why you want to move." For many students, this is the first time they have been asked to think about their community. The topic can lead them to question how they have been brought up, or how they want to bring up their children.

2. For *narration*: "Tell what happens in a day in the life of a typical suburban or urban wife, husband, son, daughter." This leads to a lively discussion of roles, as students confront the different possibilities open to them.

3. For *definition*: "Define yourself as a member of your family and show how you share values." This leads to a discussion of how individuality is expressed within a family.

4. For *description and exposition*: "Interview a member of your family and try to capture a sense of what the person is like." This topic is important for several reasons. It teaches interview and listening skills; it helps bring students closer to the family member they interview; and it enables students in the class to compare notes about their mothers, brothers, etc., and discuss how cultural factors may affect personal feelings.

5. For *comparison and contrast*: "Compare and contrast two members of your family." This leads to a discussion of the values of different generations and how children both reflect and shake off their parents' images of them.

6. For *argumentation*: "Argue about a contemporary, controversial issue affecting the family, e.g., the Equal Rights Amendment, the Human Life Amendment, the draft, with a member of your family." Discussion here centers

on how people form opinions: Do children always absorb the values of their parents? Are students' opinions more similar to those of their friends than to those of their parents?

7. For *definition and exposition*: "Analyze and explain images of people in family roles as they are pictured in advertising." I showed the film *Killing Us Softly* to illustrate images of women in advertising. It was the biggest hit of the course.

8. For a *research paper*: "Do research about the history of your family or community and show how you are either carrying on a tradition or breaking away from one." In addition to learning the different research techniques, students see the value of doing research as they try to uncover details about their own pasts. This paper also leads them to appreciate history, an insight new to most of them.

III. Evaluation

Both class discussion and student writing are enriched by this infusion of a feminist perspective into a rigid syllabus. Class discussions often turn on the definition of the family itself. While a good many of my mainly white, mainly middle-class students live in a conventional nuclear family, some live in families headed by one parent, and some live in families with a parent who has remarried. We discuss the extended European family (a good many have a grandparent living with them) as well as feminists' definition of a family as a group of close friends who may or may not live together. We discuss living with someone and not being married, as well as being married without children. Students find they are discovering something about themselves, and their papers are interesting and thoughtful. They even become interested in the writing process itself when they have an urgent need to communicate their ideas. And I find that I have in fact covered the requirements of the course syllabus and at the same time taught the class in a style that conformed to my feminist principles.

How I Would Liberate My Mother

Mickey Pearlman

I. Rationale

"Liberation" is a current buzzword which is much maligned, often misused and frequently misunderstood. Having said that, one needs to add this: the word itself and the concept behind it provide an excellent framework for a first assignment in a writing course which deals with questions of equity and feminism.

This assignment is called "How I Would Liberate My Mother" or, in some cases, "How I Would Liberate My Father In Order to Liberate My Mother." The assignment requires a thorough in-class discussion of the word "liberate." On most college campuses students still believe, initially, that "liberation" means that you drop the baby off at the day care center after you leave the maternity ward and before you show up at your law office (job at IBM, brain surgery residency, etc.) Visions of "Bra-burners" and "libbers" still dance in students' heads. The instructor must disabuse them of that tabloid definition of feminism and substitute a better one: that if a woman has chosen the patterns and the goals of her own life, even if it is the life of a traditional, home-centered woman, she does not need to be liberated from anything. "Liberate" means "to be set free," not to be kidnapped or transformed against one's will. Students need to understand that a discussion of liberation is basically a discussion of options and of choices; they are really asking if the female parent has been able to exercise her own choice.

II. Methodology

Students should begin by asking themselves the following questions:

1. Now that I know what "liberate" really means (denotation, not connotation), how can I examine the situation in my parents' home and ignore popular opinion? This is a question of equity and fairness. How can I put aside my own biases and examine the evidence?
2. How would I define the environment in which my mother lives? Perhaps there were and are not choices for her.
3. Does she need "to be set free" and from what, in *my* opinion?
4. Does she need "to be set free" and from what, in *her* opinion?
5. How would I define words like "authority" and "oppression" or "choice" and "freedom"?
6. Do I know enough about my mother's feelings and emotions in order to make a judgment?

The next step is for students to listen carefully to the answers which they receive, being equally careful *not* to edit out information which invalidates or destroys preconceived notions, or to collect only quotes which support the points they wish to make. Dozens of papers have been written on mothers who felt trapped and stifled and had been perceived as free spirits. Many an interesting essay has been submitted on a satisfied housewife who had previously been perceived as a household drudge. Students are not immune to the old Latin dictum: "Fere Libenter Homines Id Quod Volunt Credunt" (Men gladly believe what they wish to).

Instructors can help students test the degree of their prejudice, intractability or confusion on this issue by introducing the essay "I Want A Wife" by Judy Syfers. Syfers wrote this essay from a woman's point of view ("I belong to that classification of people known as wives. I Am A Wife. And, not altogether incidentally, I am a mother" (*The Heath Reader*, 20).

Her point is that if women had wives to send them through school, raise the children, plan the menus, do the grocery shopping, entertain the guests, "keep (the) clothes clean, ironed, mended . . .," and to pick up the proverbial socks, women would have the time, the energy and the freedom to study, to create and to live lives free of onerous responsibilities and full of satisfaction. As she says, after examining the benefits of a wife who takes care of one's personal, social and housekeeping problems, "My God, who *wouldn't* want a wife?"

Ironically, however, instructors who intend to explore the relationship between feminism and composition are often disappointed because classroom response to this essay is frequently undependable. Only the hardened chauvinists among us seem attracted to this vision of womanhood and wifehood. During the last six years I have watched the responses of male students and few have admitted to "wanting" this kind of "wife." Even fewer seem to think it would be possible to find this kind of wife even if they wanted her. The male students, on the average, are quick to use words like, "boring," "dull" and "outdated" in describing Syfers' married woman. If anything, they usually vie with each other in denying her attractiveness. But what often follows is the realization (and this is crucial) that if Syfers is not describing the wives they want, she is describing the mothers they already have. The male students are quick to point out that their mothers "work outside the home" and it is usually left to the female students, and to the instructor, to explain that such women now have two full-time jobs. Gathering responses for this assignment can be problematic. Students cite mothers who are unwilling to participate. Apparently, it is difficult for some mothers to share their dissatisfactions with their sons and daughters, but it should be noted that there is a paper in that too.

III. Evaluation

The issues of choice, fairness and equity, as they are related to feminism, are indivisible and crucial. However, whenever students examine stereotypes (gender, racial, religious, social, etc.) in any form (and misguided notions about "liberation" are stereotypical), three questions should be suggested or the assignment will not elicit thoughtful responses.

1. What is the current stereotypical notion of the group under discussion?
2. How do their own ideas contribute to the perpetuation of the stereotype?
3. What is the truth?

"How I Would Liberate My Mother" is an assignment which was devised to help college instructors teach students how to write by encouraging them to think and to approach the material theoretically and philosophically. This assignment also serves to introduce a four-week discussion of stereotypes ("All Jews love money," "All Irishmen drink," "Feminists are lesbians," "All housewives watch soap operas," "Black people are better basketball players," "People on welfare don't want jobs," "Frenchmen love sex," "Poles are dumb"), and, for students who participate, it is an opportunity to explore, investigate and to clarify their own answers.

Works Cited

Syfers, Judy. "I Want a Wife." In *The Heath Reader*. Ed. Boyd Litzinger. Lexington, MA: D. C. Heath and Company, 1983. 20-21.

Chapter Five

Equity Across the Curriculum: The Administrator's Challenge

This chapter addresses the challenge to writing program administrators as they attempt to cultivate equity and writing across the curriculum. The essays confront the issue of departmental politics and focus on the place of the writing specialist and administrator within the traditional departmental and university hierarchy. The section also analyzes the pedagogical biases that could compromise the success of writing across the curriculum and outlines the liberating dimensions of successful cross-curricular writing programs.

Revisionist Theory on Moral Development and its Impact Upon Pedagogical and Departmental Practice

Robert Mielke

The writing teacher or writing program administrator greets with gratitude any additional insight into the nature of hierarchies; are not our active careers divided into imposing and receiving its dubious benefits? To try to transcend such modes of structuring leads inevitably to some fiendish pedagogical *aporia*. Yet, the recent research on moral development undertaken by Carol Gilligan provides useful insight into the context of hierarchical thought in moral development, ideas which can inform our interactions with students and colleagues. Ultimately, they will even lead us to question the institution as it exists, and some of the neat counter-institutions other ideologies might seek out. Herein lies the true *aporia*: the attempt of feminist thought to articulate a new social ethos, like Mallarmé's poet bringing a new word into the language.

Carol Gilligan's investigation into moral development arose from the amazingly neglected circumstance that Freud, Erikson and Kohlberg had all formulated their respective developmental theories using solely male subjects for evidence. When she compared young male and female subjects' responses to Kohlberg's experimental ethical dilemma of whether a husband should steal an expensive drug from a pharmacist to save the life of his spouse, she found markedly different criteria involved to justify the responses. The young male subjects called upon *a priori*, abstract ethical principles to explain their decision, whatever it might be:

Transposing a hierarchy of power into a hierarchy of values, he defuses a potentially explosive conflict between people by casting it as an impersonal conflict of claims. In this way, he abstracts the moral problem from the interpersonal situation, finding in the logic of fairness an objective way to decide who will win the dispute (32).

"Higher" principles are cited to rule upon a specific case. Young women faced with this problem, on the other hand, tended to consider it as part of "a network of connection, a web of relationships that is sustained by a process of communication." The people in the problem become the basis for its solution: why won't the pharmacist yield the drug? Could he or she be persuaded to do the same? Could the husband get a loan somewhere? (28-32).

What emerges from Gilligan's research is a marvelous new way of perceiving moral growth. Both genders, in their development toward full androgynous individuation, employ the logic of both "hierarchy" and "web," but in inverse developmental paths. She sees women as moving from "web" or "network" criteria to some faith in principle, what she calls "an ethic of care," after profound personal crises which cannot be easily resolved without hurting anyone in the web of human solidarity (173-174). She uses abortion decisions as a primary example: here is a case where someone has to get hurt. Although she considers male development less thoroughly, it seems implicit that such development would occur from hierarchy to web, from faith in abstract principles to mistrust in same, as a result of a crisis which they could not satisfactorily resolve or which they were in fact responsible for, perhaps a divorce in midlife or a jail sentence.

These two ways of decision-making reflect the two major competing orientations in composition theory: the product-oriented Current-Traditionalist and process-oriented pedagogies (which include both neo-Aristotelians, who emphasize heuristic invention strategies, and the new romantics, who stress intuitive discovery).[1] We know the product-oriented classroom all too well. Students study prose novels, and attempt to come up to their level. Revise as much as you want, but turn in the paper only once for evaluation. Success lies in imitating the conventions of the universe of discourse at hand. In English, that's usually the five paragraph, "keyhole" method, Sheridan Baker special: good intro, tight thesis with at least three arguments which control the body, conclusion. The "web" of audience is unimportant. The paper has one reader, the teacher. Product-oriented pedagogy in composition emphasizes an ethic of competition for the grade, agonic struggle with peers—in short, hierarchy. At the top of the pyramid of "write stuff" resides the teacher, followed by the other individual writers, by class rank. The teacher can play good cop or bad cop; he or she can be the benevolent dictator who obviates the need for peer critiquing or the malevolent sub-hunter prowling the seas of textuality in quest of the dysfunctional student-athlete whom he or she can force to surface with an honors council case. Both kinds of Current-Traditionalists reside at most institutions.

Process-oriented teaching, contrarily, offers a non-hierarchical community of writers and readers which approximates the logic of Gilligan's "web" reasoning. The classroom will be run as a workshop: peers in small groups will offer each other feedback on drafts and revisions, writing will be taught as a recursive activity directed toward a palpable collectivity. Product usually will rear its head, for reasons cited below: the end of the semester stops the revision process, when the final portfolio of work is turned in. Depending upon the teacher, final evaluation may be done solely by the teacher, or by the peer group or indeed the writer in various conceivable combinations.

Within the process-oriented classroom, the new romantics approximate evaluation by web rather than hierarchy more closely than the neo-Aristotelians. While the latter do depict the writing act as a geometric network of some sort, for instance a triangle of language bounded by writer, audience and reality, they employ *a priori* principles about writing in their heuristics, from Aristotle's *topoi* to more new-fangled invention strategies such as the pentad, the star, particle/wave/field etc.[2] The new romantics portray every writing act as a unique Whiteheadian "event" (and, after all, isn't process teaching the offspring of process philosophy?): the best thing a teacher can do is stand back and witness the natural birth of the text, assisted by the slight vocal assistance of the peer group midwives. The recursiveness of the writing act neatly comprises my metaphor, but its organicism is appropriate for this school.

The movement from product-oriented pedagogy and neo-Aristotelianism to new-Romantic writing theory seems to follow Gilligan's paradigm for male moral development. This is not surprising, when we consider the relatively recent enfranchisement of women in the profession. But arguably, things are improving in the teaching of writing: the transition from Current-Traditionalist to neo-Aristotelian and especially new romantic pedagogies implies a shift from hierarchical to relational criteria of evaluation. Which is good news for all writers, and especially the sociologically marginal basic writer, who finds the hierarchical gameplaying of product-oriented teaching a game she cannot play to win for many complex sociological, psychological and neurological reasons. Belatedly, pedagogy is coming to embrace the web of solidarity with which the young woman begins her moral development.

I was surprised when I discovered the need for Gilligan's web not just in pedagogy, but in the administration of writing programs. I had overlooked the obvious: one of the reasons writing theorists favor initially "feminine" structures is that writing specialists are disenfranchised pseudo-administrators in the larger hierarchy of the university. Stephen M. North says it all too well in his recent article, "The Idea of a Writing Center":

> Consider . . . the pattern of writing center origins as revealed in back issues of *The Writing Lab Newsletter*: the castoff, windowless classroom (or in some cases literally, closet), the battered desks, the old textbooks, a phone (maybe), no budget, and almost inevitably, a director with limited status—an untenured or non-tenure track faculty member, a teaching assistant, an undergraduate, a "paraprofessional," etc. Now who do you suppose has determined what is to happen in that center? Not the director, surely; not the staff, if there is one. The mandate is clearly from the sponsoring body, usually an English department (437).

Even as the basic writing student is victimized by the hierarchy of his classroom, the writing instructor is the pawn of her department. Few colleagues ever put it as blatantly as the archetypal paraphraser of Clemenceau, who might aver that "the teaching of writing is too important to be left to the writing specialists." The English department teaches "literature," hence the writing specialist is the skeleton at the departmental feast. Dark double of the basic writer she teaches, she has no real power in the hierarchy.

The inevitable need for reliance on networking, appealing to the web of human connection rather than personal powers, for such an administrator should be apparent. The marginal should employ marginal strategies. Practically speaking, this may mean compromising administrative principles in the writing center in hopes of gradualist reform: tutor guidelines, for example, might prove to be an exceptionally sticky issue. Progressive writing centers would be dismayed at the qualifications frequently imposed by English departments which restrict the flexibility of writing tutors: they might only be able to examine a student draft under supervision, without a pencil, asking questions about it from a designated list, with the consent of instructor, up until the midterm on an ungraded assignment.

A second practical implication: keep all lines of communication open. For a writing program administrator, the best linkages will be extra-departmental, excepting the chairperson. The senior faculty may look askance at a junior colleague who is a powerless administrator that knows something they don't (all writing specialists really are academic subversives, for reasons below; their distrust is understandable). The chair, sundry deans, established tutor programs, and the athletic department will perceive the Writing Program's needs and benefits much better, and are hence most easily approached in relational ways when one needs specific help with specific problems.

The most surprising and specific resonance between Carol Gilligan's revisionist moral categories and our concerns as educators can be found in larger visions of the educational institution itself. As Richard Ohmann suggests in *English in America*, English departments are hierarchies within an institutional hierarchy which in turn mirrors and preserves the hierarchical structures of liberal capitalism. In mid-nineteenth

176 Mielke

century Cambridge, when Harvard changed from a school for ministers and gentlemen to a training ground for the burgeoning managerial class of the Gilded Age, rhetoricians such as Edward Tyrell Channing replaced the old Aristotelian rhetoric with Current-Traditionalist approaches. In such a rhetoric, the audience controls the orator, unlike the older school or emergent newer schools.[3] The political implications remain obvious. The instructor of English perpetuates the hegemony of the ruling elite in the hierarchical classroom. Ohmann's book concludes with the observation that pedagogical change is dependent upon political change.

Feminism's ultimate value for western discourse is its needed inquiry: what kind of change should that be? Pedagogically, what would a school built on a web model of morality look like? Ivan Illich made an early attempt at an answer, working quite independently of Gilligan, in his "Learning Webs" chapter of *Deschooling Society*. Uncannily, he anticipates her delineation of feminine modes of thought in his depiction of a society with radically decentralized learning exchanges, linked by high-tech "opportunity webs" to cater to the immediate needs of the individual learner (72-104). Such a society would run on the microstructures women have favored over the millennia and male historians have overlooked in order to study the macro-structures of church, nation and army.

Here, at least, is the promised *aporia*, the web which unravels hierarchical pattern in emulation of Penelope. If, as Antonio Gramsci stated, the goal of the intellectual must be to posit a counter-hegemony against the currently-empowered oppressors of the proletariat, the goal of the feminist intellectual must be to create a counter-hegemony which is also an anti-hegemony.[4] Marxists criticize feminism's lack of firm teleology; this may be its most radical feature. Historicist literary critics "place" feminist criticism as a subset of Marxist thought. Will the opposite arrangement prove to be the case? Although Marxism posits a non-hierarchical society, it uses agonic struggle, not nonviolent interconnection, to attain its ends. Carol Gilligan has made a first effort in expressing an overlooked ethic which has the capacity to transform our behavior as teachers and administrators.

Notes

1. For an organized exposition of writing pedagogy, see James A. Berlin, "Contemporary Composition: The Major Pedagogical Theories," *College English* 44 (December, 1982): 765-777.

2. A typical "communications triangle" can be found in Kenneth Dowst, "The Epistemic Approach: Writing, Knowing, and Learning," *Eight Approaches to Teaching Composition*, Eds. Timothy R. Donovan and Ben W. McClelland (Urbana, IL: National Council of Teachers of English, 1980), 65- Ben W. McClelland explains copiously invention strategies like the pentad, star, particle/wave/field in *Writing Practice: A Rhetoric of the Writing Process* (New York: Longman, 1984), 23-56.

3. Richard Ohmann, *English in America: A Radical View of the Profession* (New York: Oxford University Press, 1976), 215; Wallace Douglas, "Rhetoric for the Meritocracy" in Ohmann, 116. Every composition teacher should also read chapter 7 in this work (172-206), which shows how well the Pentagon Papers conform to the standards we set in composition writing.

4. It remains an interesting question: which school of Marxism is most congenial to feminist thought? To some extent, all are save Leninism and the later Lukacs, with their very hierarchical concept of "democratic centralism," a revolutionary party in power. Rosa Luxembourg and Bakunin, with their interest in spontaneous revolution which spawned the New Left are more acceptable, as are the Frankfurt School with their disdain for the distortions of popular culture, which feminists share for intersecting reasons. I find Antonio Gramsci useful as applied above. There is no substitute for actually reading *Selections from the Prison Notebooks* and *Letters from Prison*, but interested parties who want a glance at his ideas on hegemony and the role of the intellectual should consult ch. IX in James Joll, *Antonio Gramsci* (New York: Viking Press, 1978), 117-134.

Works Cited

Gilligan, Carol. *In A Different Voice: Psychological Theory and Women's Development.* Cambridge, MA: Harvard University Press, 1982.

Illich, Ivan. *Deschooling Society.* New York: Harper and Row, 1971.

North Stephen M. "The Idea of a Writing Center." *College English* 46 (1984): 433-446.

Why Teaching Writing Always Brings Up Questions of Equity

Judith Bechtel

Students at our university have access to a wonderful filmstrip about discrimination called "The Tale of O" (Goodmeasure, 1978). The whole filmstrip is done symbolically with X's depicting the majority or the dominant group and O's representing the minority or subordinate group. Although the production is designed for businesses that are beginning to integrate Blacks, women or some other minority group into the mainstream of their activities, you can also use the filmstrip as a statement about composition instruction within the university curriculum. In fact, there are many reasons why composition specialists (or English faculty members who like to teach writing) might consider themselves O's within a field of X's.

In the filmstrip, the dominant X's do not become conscious that they are a group until the arrival of some O's. They are so used to seeing only each other and speaking about their own issues in their own jargon that they wrongly assume they are the total reality. Their preconceptions, in other words, are assumed and unanalyzed. A parallel in English departments has the X's as literary scholars, and their focus has become refined and highly polished works of art. They have other preconceptions, too, depending on the school of criticism emphasized where the professors were graduate students, but in general their focus of attention was on the text and not on the student. These X's by and large are understandably baffled by the texts produced by their inexperienced students in comparison with the literary masters. And the arrival of a group of O's, those of us trained in the teaching of the writing process (as opposed to the interpretation of a finished piece of professional writing) have made the literature specialists conscious that they have a bias.

Indeed, the teaching of writing challenges many, if not most, of the traditional assumptions about pedagogy. It can't be done by lecturing; it must make use of talking, small groups, collaboration, and other methods of sharing the power within the classroom. From the very beginning of interest in the process approach to teaching writing (which I date back to Janet Emig's *The Composing Processes of Twelfth Graders* in 1971), there has been a recognition that learning to write had to involve a personal, organic, discovery-centered way of operating. Often the people attracted to learning about the teaching of writing were in themselves different sorts of people than those attracted to literary studies—or even to the analysis of rhetoric or to linguistics. Often the people who like to have their students move their chairs into circles rather than keeping them in straight rows tended to be more radical, more open, more adventuresome than their colleagues, the X's.

Actually, quite a few of the original O's were women! It might seem a natural development for women to dedicate themselves to the "servicing" of the English departments, the doing of the person-centered developmental work that English composition represents, the meticulous correction of all those themes. In many departments, including my own, the administration of writing programs was also relegated to women almost by default. Most professors simply did not want that kind of thankless work. Other minority O's relegated to the teaching of composition include the much overworked graduate assistant and the much exploited part-time instructor (whose stories of exploitation are worthy of a fuller discussion of academic morality in the midst of fiscal pressures). In short, one measure of the low prestige that writing instruction represents is the rank and salary level of those who teach writing.

Of course, men are also attracted to the ranks of writing instructors, but it is my contention that most of these are unusual men amongst their academic peers: gentler, less ambitious, more playful. Those men who do not fit this stereotype frequently go in for hard research or publication or other outlets which are more traditionally recognized at promotion and tenure time.

Which brings up yet another sad, but relevant fact regarding the portrayal of writing instructors as O's in a field of X's— that is their frequent difficulties in attaining tenure. For all of the reasons cited above—because they teach differently, because they labor heroically (with students instead of with literary scholarship), and because they tend to come from the ranks of the invisible (women, part-time instructors, etc.), they are often hard to measure against the traditional standards. This problem is confounded by the natural defensiveness of an entrenched group whose very preconceptions are being identified and challenged and so are in need of being "defended"—thus all the talk of standards as a rationale for exclusion on promotion and tenure.

Talk of standards brings up further ramifications of the issue of equity in composition instruction—and that is equity from the students' point of view—treatment received and grades received being the measure of their fair treatment. Students, it must be pointed out, are often the victims of the inequities of prestige, status, and budgeting that affect the staffing of writing classes. Although I have described writing instructors as an identifiable group within the academic community, they are so only to the extent that they are aware of and responsive to the last twenty years of composition research and its implications. Let's face it, many of the people who teach writing are really just X's who have not lucked out. They may be waiting to earn the right to teach literature, or they may be forced into the ranks of the writing specialist (even to part-time status) by necessity rather than by choice. Understandably, some of these people are bitter as well as ineffective, and sometimes they perpetuate unhealthy rituals of ridicule and redmarking that keep their students from full development as writers. Inequities within the system inevitably affect most the clientele at the bottom of the heap.

It is ironic that so many aspects of discrimination should exist around writing instruction since writing itself can be such a liberating experience. When writing is taught as a mode of learning (Emig, 1977; Bechtel, 1985), then students experience writing as a joyful and ego-affirming process. Needless to say, that attitude toward writing promotes an egalitarian world-view, one in which all people, not just a few artists, are potential writers. Just as a richer blend of people (women, Blacks, other minorities) enrich the environment of businesses in "The Tale of O," so the addition of process-centered composition instructors enrich the academic environment. Within systems which have been traditionally elitist, authoritarian, and hierarchical, composition research and instruction has brought new patterns of sharing power, new possibilities for collaboration rather than competition.

It is no coincidence that the advent of such a challenge is linked to questions of equity. "The Tale of O" itself was created in response to the tensions and conflicts that characterized early efforts at integrating the workforce, particularly at the managerial level. Many of the tensions depicted are also characteristics of English departments in transition. The first O's hired are always "Super O's," for they know they are tokens whose behavior and performance will affect hiring later. However, this high performance level of initial composition specialists hired may have several untoward effects. First, the workload exhausts the person hired, who often ends up discouraged, if not derailed. Second, it sets up an expectation that all such specialists should be similarly extraordinary, and thus subsequent hirees are viewed as a disappointment. And finally, it allows for a good guy/bad guy phenomenon later when the second such specialist is seen as different. One or the other of them, because they are in the minority, will be denied tenure, will be given an onerous teaching load, or in some other way be discriminated against. In the meantime, the writing specialist will be presumed to be an apologist for the profession, an allegiance he or she may choose (for practical purposes) to minimize. In short, the tension-filled period of transition will inevitably be a time for raising equity questions. The O's will always be conscious that they do not look like X's until such time as our departments of English truly integrate, serving students in the beginning stages of their college years as well as graduate students, offering courses with varied pedagogies to be taught by professionals with legitimate claims to tenure and prestige.

Works Cited

Bechtel, Judith A. *Improving Writing and Learning.* Boston: Allyn and Bacon, 1985.

Emig, Janet. "Writing as a Mode of Learning." *College Composition and Communication* 28 (May 1977): 122-128.

————. *The Composing Processes of Twelfth Graders.* Urbana, IL: National Council of Teachers of English, 1971.

Wheatley, Meg, et al. "The Tale of O." Filmstrip prepared by Goodmeasure Consultants, 1978.

Writing Across the Curriculum: a Model for a Workshop and a Call for Change

Cynthia L. Caywood and Gillian R. Overing

Recently we were invited to lead a workshop for chairpeople on writing across the curriculum at a small liberal arts university. We were asked because we had both been researching and employing new, nontraditional approaches to teaching writing. Our primary objective was to impress upon this diverse group their responsibility for encouraging and improving writing skills across the campus. We also felt that it was equally important to stimulate their interest in the writing process as many of them were unfamiliar with writing as a distinct discipline. As process teachers we believe in the dynamism and potential for growth inherent in the workshop approach to teaching writing, and we structured the chairpeople's workshop accordingly. We simulated, as closely as possible (given the time limit) the developmental aspects of both teaching and learning fostered by the workshop methods we employ in our classrooms. We used small group work, collaboration, model critiquing, reader-response and the principles of Socratic dialogue. We met our primary goal; interest was keen and concern was high. However, the two days of discussion and interaction prompted us to consider larger and more troubling questions which fundamentally challenge the traditional, hierarchically-structured basis of the student/teacher relationship.

Twenty-five people participated in the workshop; this number included chairpeople and administrators; of this group five were women, and all were senior faculty members. We divided the workshop into three main sessions, interspersed with coffee, cocktails, and meals. (These interim social gatherings emerged as very important, for they encouraged informal revealing responses to the workshop sessions, and we shall discuss these later.) What follows will be a description of the workshop format, our evaluation of the participants' responses, and a concluding discussion of the far-reaching implications as they bear upon pedagogical theory and questions of equity.

Session I: The Writing Process

To recreate for the chairpeople the actual classroom experience, we asked them to assume the role of a student in a writing class.

Stage 1: The Writing Profile

We announced that we would divide the group into smaller groups of five. In order to achieve a balance of abilities within each group, we asked all the participants to compose a profile of their writing abilities. The profiles could take the form of a list of strengths and weaknesses, descriptive notes, personal opinions, comments and criticisms they had received from journal editors, comments their high school or college teachers had made (good and bad!); in short, we requested as much information as they would give us in the form that they found most accessible. We also suggested that, as part of the role-assumption process, they could assume a role if they wished: that of a poor or excellent writer, a different persona, etc. We stressed that engaging in and understanding the workshop process was the most important part of the exercise. We collected the profiles while the participants were engaged in stage two.

As we expected, the profiles were assessments of "standard" writing abilities such as spelling, punctuation, paragraph ordering, logic, wordiness, organization, clarity, etc., which varied from one individual to the next. But there were also some repeated observations and complaints about lack of creativity and motivation:

-motivation is a weakness, writing is a chore

-proclivity for polysyllabic words for their own sake

-tendency to write in a "stodgy" way in order to be technically correct

-tendency to blandness

-my writing is almost always "academic"

-my writing tends to be grammatically correct, but turgid

-I can communicate adequately, but not elegantly

-lack of creativity

-I write as if I were giving a lecture or a public address; therefore, I have difficulty developing a more literary form of writing.

These comments revealed some interesting underlying patterns. First, writing is unpleasant. It is also rigidly divided into two kinds: creative (elegant, colorful, literary) and academic (utilitarian, disciplined, mundane, but nevertheless, more valuable). The absolute split between creativity and scholarship, or, to put it another way, between style and content, suggests to us a habit of mind that is categorizing, structured and comparative. In other words, many of the participants did not view writing as thinking, but rather as transcription; they assumed that style is a mere embellishment, that correctness atones for turgidity, and that what is valued is not the process but the product.

Stage 2: Paragraph Assignment: "How do you grade?"

In order to get a writing sample for their group work, we handed out dittos and requested that they write for twenty minutes on "How I grade." We emphasized that they could approach this assignment in the way that they felt most comfortable; it could be a description of their ideal grading environment (for example, "I always require a certain place, certain light, certain pen, a cup of coffee, a glass of Scotch," etc.), or it could be an analysis of their grading process, criteria, and methodology. We chose this topic because we had planned to discuss the grading of writing the next day and also simply because we knew grading to be a common experience. Some characteristic comments were:

-The grading process, as I practice it, consists of the following steps: a re-study, by me, of the material on which the examination was rendered, a reading of each exam paper to evaluate how nearly the student provided the information or analysis requested. . . .

-Having formulated a good question I now formulate what I consider to be a perfect answer and proceed to read the students' papers against this backdrop.

-I always put comments for outstanding work to reinforce positively and try not to be too deprecating or sarcastic for inferior work.

-During the day on which the test is given, I try to read over several papers with no view toward making any specific evaluation. The purpose of this cursory examination is to form an impression of how well or poorly the students performed. . . .

-I begin the grading process by deciding first how much weight to give each problem, and this may be affected by the initial reading mentioned earlier.

-I begin by working the exam and taking excursions in the problem-solving which may not be correct but which some students inevitably take. I then award points on the basis of progress in the solution of the problem rather than on an all-or-nothing basis. High credit is given to ingenuity even though the final result may be in error.

-To my surprise, the papers are generally interesting, sometimes provocative and oftentimes let me know my students are learning to see and enjoy art.

Again, surveying these paragraphs, we detected some consistent principles at work. Many of the participants posited the existence of an ideal text, against which the student's singular response was measured. The author of that ideal text was usually the teacher. With this approach, teachers assumed a power that, as the third quotation would indicate, may be overextended. Other participants were less hierarchical in their grading, evolving standards out of student texts under scrutiny. With these teachers a greater emphasis was placed on process; and while there were judgments to be made, the instructor also learned from the students. These differing approaches extend the earlier division from writing as process.

Stage 3: A Model Critique

When the participants had completed Stage 2, we dittoed off their writing samples, gave out group assignments, and offered them a model critique of a student paragraph. We role-played teacher and student, acting out the reader-response basis of our interaction with students in a one-on-one conference. The paragraph we chose was particularly weak which allowed us to suggest the range of possible responses from mechanical errors to evaluation and revision of content. Our model critique served as an humorous, perhaps somewhat caricatured, example of what we wanted them to do in their groups.

Stage 4: Group Critiques

We had attempted to put the participants in groups that reflected their writing strengths and weaknesses, and also matched more apparently gregarious individuals with quieter ones. We placed one woman in each group. Urging them to begin, we left the room briefly, and returned to circulate quietly, listening in and occasionally offering observations.

The participants responded to group work much as our composition students do for the first time. One person assumed a leadership role and attempted to move the group along. Nervous laughter frequently erupted; some groups energetically and eagerly pursued the task, others required more urging and direction from us. Also familiar to us were the hurt and defensive tones of someone who felt her or his work was being roughly treated. The purpose of Stage 4 was to recreate for the participants the student classroom context with its attendant personality dynamics and potential vulnerabilities. Just as we had asked them in Stage 1 to examine themselves as writers (a new examination for some), in Stage 4 we asked them to refamiliarize themselves with the position of being a student. We observed that many of the participants were uncomfortable with what they perceived as the powerlessness of their situation. They were reluctant to be judged by peers, whom they did not perceive as experts. Additionally, they were disturbed by the apparent lack of hierarchical structure inherent in the equitability of group work, where there is no recourse to single authority. Once again these were responses we had frequently encountered with our composition students. We recognized that the powerlessness that the participants were experiencing as students might have been ratified or understandable to them as teachers if there had been a perceived, accountable authority. But beyond the predictability of bewilderment and disturbed sensibilities, the participants' responses opened up another dimension of analysis. We see a continuation of the patterns established in Stages 1 and 2. The need for structure and a source of authority in the classroom parallels the adherence to the notion of an ideal text (whether essay or exam answer), which in turn results in a concern with product and an indifference to process.

Session II: Evaluating Student Writing

This session was devoted to reading and evaluating writing. Our premise was that before teachers can help students become better writers, they must understand the composing process and allow students the opportunity to revise.

Stage 1: Understanding the Process

We distributed a student paragraph to the participants, one which showed potential and originality, but was nevertheless weak. Participants then critiqued it and pointed out its weaknesses and strengths. The author had been asked to talk to himself and describe his writing process. A transcript of this taped monologue was then distributed.

Initially, participants' responses were highly critical, often condescending, and largely proscriptive. With the reading of the transcript, what became apparent were the difficulties the student was facing as a writer: his obsessive concern with correct spelling and style, the ways in which the assignment and the time in which to complete it were limiting him, and his fear of offending the person whom he was describing. This information made it possible to understand the paragraph's weaknesses and discover ways of improving it, and changed dramatically the participants' responses. They became sympathetic and constructively critiqued the particular strengths and weaknesses of the writer rather than proscriptively addressing the problems of the text. They concerned themselves with what the writer was doing rather than with what he was failing to do. They were beginning to identify the importance of process.

Stage 2: Putting the Process to Work

Here we discussed meaningful teacher response. Informing the group that "we have scarcely a shred of empirical evidence to show that students typically even comprehend our responses to their writing, let alone use them purposefully to modify their practice" (Knoblauch and Brannon, 1-4), we argued that the problem was not that students were indifferent to teacher commentary. Rather, we argued that the problem originated in the kinds of comments made and the lack of opportunity students had to act upon them.

We then distributed two copies of a single essay. We had marked one with more traditional, proscriptive suggestions; in the other we had tried to indicate reader response through questions which pointed to the student's failure to communicate. For example, typical marginalia on the first attacked grammar mistakes and sentence errors, and suggested the break-up and reorganization of paragraphs; the final comment urged that the student pay more attention to structure, clarity, and proof-reading. In contrast, the marginalia of the second essay posed questions about content and outlined specific difficulties the reader was having in accepting or understanding the points. The final comment on the second essay posed larger questions about the general argument and urged attention be given to any recurrent grammatical problems. The end result, we argued, would be that students would be forced to rethink the problem and hence revise meaningfully rather than just tidying the essay up. The participants quickly saw the point and responded enthusiastically.

Stage 3: Watching the Process Work

In demonstration of our suggestions about meaningful teacher response, we offered them the first and second drafts of a student narrative taken from one of our classes. In contrast to earlier samples of student writing, the first draft, or the "before" stage was competent, articulate, and relatively error-free. The debate over the relative merits of these drafts was lively and involved some controversy. We include them for the reader's appraisal:

First Draft

As I maneuvered the car into the parking spot 300 ft. from the dunes, my mind was full of turmoil. It was the last day of my summer; the next day I was to leave for college. It is hard for me to say why I was disappointed. After all, tomorrow I was going to embark on an adventure lasting four years, which would change my entire life. But, where had the summer gone? It seemed as if yesterday I was speaking at commencement but it had actually been three whole months. I had worked all summer except for these last two weeks which I spent with my girlfriend at the beach. Today was my last day to spend with her, so I planned to make it special.

The day was one of the hottest this summer. The ocean's strong breeze lessened the intensity of the noontime heat. The short shadows played on the weather beaten fence which followed an inconsistent path across the surrounding dunes. The screeching of the gulls and the crashing of the waves combined to complete the setting I had envisioned.

Through my efforts to make this last day unforgettable for her, I had somehow kept it all a secret. Until this very moment, she still had no idea what I had planned. However, as I went around to the truck and began to get our things, she caught a glimpse of the wicker picnic basket hidden there. Her surprise was evident by the immediate smile and sparkle in her eyes. As we made our unhurried ascent up the dunes with me carrying the basket I was searching for an isolated spot to picnic where we could be alone. A small clearing, shaded and enclosed, seemed perfect.

We trudged across the sand and grass, oblivious to the bushes scratching our legs. While she took off her sneakers, I began to spread the red and white checkered tablecloth on the sand. At the sight of this and the picnic lunch I set out she inquired, "Why haven't you done this before?" I smiled and said, "If I had done it before then it wouldn't seem so special now."

We enjoyed the lunch of fresh sour dough bread, dijon mustard, warm baked chicken, and a bottle of red wine. We both did our best to avoid any subjects concerning my departure for school. However, after a while the pleasant conversation became forced. It was obvious that we were avoiding certain sensitive areas. Neither of us seemed willing to stop the charade.

The drive back home was silent. We both knew that it was over for now and that things would change. The goodbyes were short because neither of us wanted to break down in front of the other.

My feelings of disappointment, however, did not lessen the excitement I felt about going to college. I realized the importance of a college education and I knew that I would grow in many ways.

Second Draft

The day was one of the hottest this summer. The ocean's strong breeze lessened the intensity of the late morning heat. Short shadows played on the weather beaten fence which followed an inconsistent path across the surrounding dunes. The screeching of the gulls and the crashing of the waves combined to complete this perfect setting.

Noontime came, signaling the busiest time at the beach. I was surprised not to see the couple which had been sunning themselves near me every day for the past two weeks. They seemed like nice enough kids, polite and not wild like so many young people are nowadays. The boy usually made a point of speaking to me. Out of our short pleasant conversations I knew that he was going to some college down south at the end of the summer. He was mighty excited just telling me about it. The girl was shy and she usually just stood there while we talked. They were always on the beach by 11:00 at the latest, so it occurred to me that he might have left for school.

Just after these thoughts had passed through my mind, the kids came into view walking arm in arm. Today, they were walking carrying a picnic basket. This was surprising, usually they went up to the "burger hut" and got their lunch. They were also quieter than usual as they crossed the sand headed for their favorite spot. I waved but they were engaged in thought and didn't see me.

As the girl took off her sweatshirt, revealing her bathing suit, her mind was elsewhere. The usual effervescent personality was replaced with a sadness which could be detected by the way she stared out at the ocean unsmiling. Every so often her gloomy gaze shifted to him.

While she sat immobile, he set out the picnic lunch. His usual self-assured, fluid movements were instead, clumsy and erratic. He was generally patient and even tempered but, today he got into a fit of anger when the wind made it impossible to keep the red and white checkered tablecloth down.

They ate staring at each other saying very little. The aroma of warm baked chicken and dijon mustard made me wish that I had been included. Their peaceful meal was only broken once, when he became frustrated trying to open a bottle of red wine.

After they finished eating it was as if a bond between the two had been broken. They purposefully avoided each other's looks and could have been mistaken as strangers by a passerby. The boy silently repacked the lunch while the girl gathered her things. As they walked off the beach their minds were busy contemplating separate thoughts.

It was apparent by the obvious detail which went to planning the lunch that the day was special. The changes in the personalities of each individual indicated that it was a stressful, sad and unsure time. The next day there was no sign of either of them. If my assumptions are correct they won't be back, yesterday being their farewell lunch together.

First we offered the participants our analysis and the ways in which we thought the second draft was superior to the first. We explained that our criticisms had been posed to the student as questions; therefore he himself had diagnosed many of the problems and been receptive to our suggestions for revisions. As mechanical errors were relatively few in the piece, the conference was directed at making the narrative into a more interesting original essay. Our criticisms focused on the overuse of cliches ("but where had the summer gone?" "I had planned to make it special;" "I would grow in many ways,") and the resultant opacity of detail; the ways in which the first person voice confined the writer's point of view and occasionally produced a smug or complacent tone; the predictability of both the situation and the familiarity of the feeling involved; the pointed moralizing, and the overly structured organization of the piece into formal components of introduction, body, and resolution. Our suggestions for revision provided a strategy for addressing and eliminating these problems. We first recommended that the writer change his point of view. This would give him a fresh new look at his own situation, forcing a keener awareness of detail. We also suggested that he begin and end where his narrative did; that the explanation provided by the introduction and conclusion might not be necessary if the details of his story were more carefully and accurately recorded. We felt that the second draft, told from the point of view of an observant old man watching the young lovers' farewell picnic, was a significant turnaround and avoided many of the original problems.

We expected a variety of responses to our assessment, and we also had some direct challenges to our judgment. Some thought the first was better than the second, and we made note of some of their comments:

-"I don't care for all the details: they're distracting and flowery."
-"I preferred the formal introduction and conclusion."
-"I liked the analysis at the end of the first one; it made the point clear."
-"I preferred the first person voice; it seemed more direct."
-"I thought the second was overly subtle."

While we appreciate that some responses were a matter of personal taste, we can once again discover some recurrent patterns: a preference for a distinct and authoritative voice; a belief that style is not as important as content and is separable from it; the opinion that immediately perceptible clarity is better than a less structured, more organic approach to the subject in question.

Session III: Writing at the University

The final session was a brief discussion of writing at the university itself, which was led by the chairperson of the English department. He discussed the range of students admitted to the university and the methods by which they were placed into remedial, standard, or advanced writing courses (or, exempted from composition in the case of a few). Next he presented the results of an Academic Planning Subcommittee survey, which indicated that few faculty members understood what the English department attempted in its writing courses; nor did they accept any responsibility for the teaching of writing. He offered statistics on how much writing goes on in the average composition classroom and how that translates into the number of teaching hours spent grading and conferring. Next he offered two writing samples from a fifth-year senior who, nearly illit-erate when first admitted, had been tutored weekly in the department's writing center for four years. The two samples, one taken from his first year, the other written just prior to the workshop, demonstrated dramatic improvement, but indicated that the student was still writing substandard English. On the basis of this presentation, the chairperson argued that the English department was doing its best as a vanguard of literacy and that it was the responsibility of the rest of the university faculty to promote just as vigorously writing excellence amongst the student body.

We then offered ways of incorporating more writing into their classrooms, urging that writing could be encouraged without adding to their grading load. We recommended that they require their students to keep reading journals; as an addition or alternative, they should incorporate writing exercises into the classes themselves. These exercises, we suggested, could take the form of responses to reading assignments or to lectures. We also urged that frequent short papers be assigned rather than long-term projects; or, that if a term project were preferred, that it be broken down into steps, with the teacher frequently intervening as the students drafted their papers and revised them. We specifically urged that revision be incorporated into the classroom. The teacher could take responsibility for reading drafts, or, even better, class time could be devoted to well-structured, small group reviews of work in progress. This procedure would result not only in better essays, but in sharing ideas and considering relevant points not brought up by the teacher.

Overall Evaluation

The workshop was very successful. The participants were enthusiastic and motivated to assume a new-found responsibility for maintaining writing standards at the university. As one participant said in reference to the fifth-year senior's substandard writing sample: "I'm not an expert, but I have a moral obligation to do something for this kind of student." For us as leaders, however, the workshop opened up more questions than it resolved. Some of the questions were initially brought up in the social occasions that prefaced or followed sessions. As we said earlier, these occasions fostered more informal and revealing responses to the sessions. One of the participants, who had been most uncomfortable in the group sessions, raised the key question: "Wouldn't students take it [i.e., group work] better coming from a young woman?" implying that the absence of a clear authority figure would be more acceptable in a woman's classroom. This suggestion led us to examine initially the connections between teaching methodologies and gender and eventually the more far-reaching implications of the relation of pedagogical theory to questions of equity.

We began our personal evaluation with an examination of the way feminist values are translated into pedagogical theory. We reviewed current theories about the writing process itself.[1] To speak generally and to oversimplify, writing is viewed as either an analytical or an intuitive process. If teachers begin from the analytical viewpoint, they assume that there are distinct steps in the composing process, and that these can be analyzed, classified, and taught. Writing is consequently a climb up those steps, moving towards assembling the ideal text that lies out there, somewhere beyond the topic—in the writing or thinking of the teacher or some other designated expert. Compatible with this approach in the writing classroom is the use of prose models or other ideal texts, which are so appointed because they clearly and fitly embody the envisioned peak of the writer's climb. They are models for organization, structure and rhetorical strategy that can be learned and imposed like a grid upon the amorphous mass of a student's thought, giving it form and hence meaning. This approach posits the existence of an authority—the ideal text—and a reader/judge (teacher) who measures the gap between real (student text) and ideal (imagined text). What is of greatest importance here is the finished, correct product. If the climb is correctly accomplished, the students qualify as authorities, demonstrating the regenerative capacity of hierarchical structures.

In the intuitive approach, less emphasis is placed upon the product and more is given to the process. Form grows out of meaning rather than meaning out of form. That is, the "amorphous mass" of the student's thought generates its own forms and develops structures appropriate to its content and purpose. This kind of development and discovery of meaning through the evolution of the text frees the student's thought and text. No longer is the grid of authoritative models imposed or even appropriate. Accordingly there is no ideal text. And, as there is no ideal text, there is no reader/judge. Rather, the teacher is first and foremost a collaborator. What is of greatest importance in the teacher-student relationship is the shared process of discovery which is possible only in the act of writing and the act of being read. Authority and model are abandoned for facilitator and process. This less-structured, less rigidly hierarchical, revalued, collaborative, open-ended approach is compatible with feminism, if not feminist in and of itself. Therefore we conclude that the approach to writing itself is a feminist concern.

Some of the recurrent patterns of response that we traced throughout our discussion and evaluation of the workshop correlate clearly with the former traditional, hierarchical approach to writing. We have noted the same connection between structured pedagogical approaches and rigidly hierarchical thinking amongst our colleagues and participants in subsequent workshops we have given. This connection is thrown into clear relief when teachers resolve to move from one pedagogical mode to another. For example, when establishing a workshop system in the writing classroom, teachers often experience initial anxiety due to apparent loss of control. This anxiety is sometimes displaced into a concern with classroom chaos, a belief that they are dodging the responsibility of authoritative presentation of sanctioned material, or the fear that students are not learning information that is easily or readily measurable. Sometimes the source of anxiety is candidly recognized as the loss of student attention. The teacher is no longer on center stage. In our experience most teachers get past this anxiety. They welcome the new-found energy and potential in both themselves as teachers and in their students and often find that their classrooms are revitalized.

When we undertook to conduct the workshop, we had thought that our primary objective was to impress upon this diverse group their responsibilities for encouraging and improving writing skills across the campus. In retrospect we learned that a far greater challenge lay in urging revaluation of the approach to teaching itself. Our invitation to create a more cooperative dynamic in the classroom, though it may undermine the traditional notion of the teacher's authority, fosters a greater respect for the student, a more equitable classroom, and critical independence and creativity in the student. Such an invitation is, in effect, a call for change.

Notes

1. Some texts restudied were: Sheridan Baker, *The Complete Stylist and Handbook*, 2nd ed. (New York: Harper and Row, 1980); Ann E. Berthoff, *The Making of Meaning: Metaphors, Models and Maxims for Writing Teachers* (Montclair, NJ: Boynton/Cook Publishers, Inc. 1981); Lil Brannon, Melinda Knight, and Vera Neverow-Turk, *Writers Writing* (Montclair, NJ: Boynton/Cook Publishers, Inc. 1983); Ben W. McClelland, *Writing Practice: A Rhetoric of the Writing Process* (New York: Longman, 1984); Donald Murray, *Learning by Teaching: Selected Articles on Writing and Teaching* (Montclair, NJ: Boynton/Cook Publishers, Inc. 1982); and Gary Tate and Edward P. J. Corbett, Eds., *The Writing Teacher's Sourcebook* (New York: Oxford University Press, 1981).

Works Cited

C. H. Knoblauch and Lil Brannon. "Teacher Commentary on Student Writing: The State of the Art." *Freshman English News* No. 2 (Fall, 1981): 1-4.

Women and Writing Across the Curriculum: Learning and Liberation

Rebecca Blevins Faery

For some years now I have been teaching writing at Hollins College in Virginia. For the past few years much of my energy has gone into developing a cross-curricular writing program because I believe, along with most other members of my profession, that students both learn better and learn to write better when occasions to write are given them often, in all areas of study. I've been lucky to have had cooperation and support from many of my colleagues in disciplines throughout the college, and while we have a long way to go to achieve the kind of writing program we would think ideal, we have in truth come a long way.

Hollins is a women's college, and many of our faculty feel especially committed to the education of women—that is, educating women about their history, their literature, their political situation, their place in the world. But in the past few years, as our program in writing across the curriculum has developed, we at Hollins have also begun to think about the ways in which teaching women and teaching writing are related. As a result of our ongoing conversations with each other as well as our experiences with having students write more in our courses, some of us have come to believe that there are political and feminist implications in the ways teachers throughout the college foster the language-learning and language-using of our women students.

In an interview a few years ago on the subject of "Rhetoric for Women," Wayne Booth asserted that the process of educa-

tion for women must be different from that for men, at least
as long as the situations of the two sexes in society differ.
Bringing rhetoric in as an active principle, Booth advised
women to develop rhetorical arts "to combat reductive metaphors," and to address themselves to the "reconstitution of
selves by a vigorous criticism of metaphors" and the "reconstitution of *circumstances* by a vigorous criticism of *metaphors
for situations*" (34, emphasis mine). When I began to think
about a college-wide writing program designed especially for
women students, I remembered the Booth interview as suggesting just the task I wanted to undertake: to explore the possibilities offered by the new writing pedagogy for revising the
educational circumstances of women students, and of creating
new metaphors, or redefining old ones, for the situations in
which women's learning takes place, for what happens in the
classroom between student and teacher, student and student.

The task of reconstituting metaphors for teaching and learning both fueled the development of the cross-curricular writing
program at Hollins and offered a political justification for interested faculty to reshape our teaching styles and the atmosphere of our classrooms. The process of redefining the metaphors for the learning situation had begun for me as I had
learned from many people—James Britton, Nancy Martin, Peter Elbow, John Warnock, Carl Klaus, Cleo Martin, Richard
Lloyd-Jones, and others—to think about teaching writing in
new ways. As my colleagues and I tried to make our teaching
more student-centered, we found that the strategies of the new
approach to using writing to learn suited perfectly our aim of
getting students to be more active participants in the process
of their own education. This we saw as particularly important
for women students, to help them overcome the tendencies toward passivity and intellectual dependence and timidity which
are their cultural heritage. We found that creating situations in
which students are called upon to become articulate by writing
frequently about a variety of subjects and for a variety of purposes and audiences allows them to gain faith in their ability to
deal with the world through language. They learn to create
meaning, to shape their identities and their sense of themselves, to discover who they are, how language in their envi-

ronment shapes them, and finally how they themselves can come to control their own lives through the powerful force which is language.

At Hollins, a series of seminars for our faculty on the teaching of writing, held every year since 1980, has produced a core of teachers in a number of disciplines committed to emphasizing writing in the courses they teach. It isn't difficult to convince most teachers that students should write—writing is after all one of the Three R's. It is more difficult to help teachers sustain over time the commitment to ask more writing of students. The task becomes easier if, in a thoughtful program of faculty development, teachers are given the opportunity and the time to reconsider the ways writing can make learning easier for students. Our seminars have emphasized the "writing to learn" approach and have made available to historians, biologists, musicians, poets and scholars of literature the best recent research on the value of making use of the stages of the writing process to further students' learning the subject matter of the course. We encourage teachers to bring into the classroom students' exploration, gathering of information, drafting, getting responses from several readers, revising, and finally editing, because attention to writing is, after all, attention to thinking. Certainly no one in any discipline will feel encouraged to make writing central to the activity of a course in order to "help the English department get its job done." But when teachers come to understand that students learn more literature, calculus, art, or physics when they write, and that students' writing can become a hub for all the learning activity in a classroom, they see that there is something in it for them as well.

So on our campus, writing is in the air: students in an art class write careful directions to a place and then draw a corresponding map of the area in order to study the difference between verbal and visual language. Students in a French class, preparing for a year of study in France, write letters to each other, in French, about what they hope to do and see in Paris, what they imagine life will be like for them there, what they will need to know and do to make their year abroad a success. In a sociology course, students conduct interviews of family members, friends, or people in the community and then write up the interviews for class discussion, as an introduction to doing first-hand research. Students in beginning-level literature classes write frequent short papers offering their responses to what they have read and making connections between the reading and their own experience. Student physicists in a course on "The Physics of Armageddon" do a series of drafts and revisions in preparing position papers for a public forum on nuclear weapons and global survival.

Above all, students in these courses are constantly being invited into active participation in the ongoing business of the course, even of the discipline. They are asked not just to watch teachers perform, but to behave like us, to become people who think, say, and do. It is in that sense that a curriculum which stresses writing offers particular rewards for women students and their teachers.

The revolution in writing pedagogy and the new emphasis on writing throughout the college curriculum has accompanied a more general shift of mode in education, has in fact been an integral and even motivating part of that shift. The traditional practice being challenged is one in which the student is frequently a passive recipient, the teacher is the transmitter of sacred texts and established cultural values, and language use consists of recitation, testing, and writing papers which are too often regurgitative, proof that the student has read the books, listened to the lectures, done the homework. The words are another version of someone else's. By contrast, in the new model, teacher and student are equally active. Both teacher and student assume that knowledge is, in the process of being rediscovered, undergoing revision and transformation. And language use, to borrow James Moffett's phrase, constitutes "real authoring," and does not serve only to test the student's attentiveness or preparedness. Instead, language is the means for the student to make for herself a world she can inhabit comfortably, where she can claim for herself the power of articulation, the power of control over her own reality and over others' expression of her reality.

As women have written hauntingly and repeatedly, silence is powerlessness. For male students the experience of enforced passivity during the period of their education may not be harmful; at least we know it does not serve permanently to shut them up. For women, however, the passive student role can reinforce the intellectual passivity which women are encouraged to adopt. "Listen to the silences," Adrienne Rich tells us:

> Listen to the small soft voices, often courageously trying to speak up, voices of women taught early that tones of confidence, challenge, anger, or assertiveness, are strident and unfeminine. Listen to the voices of the women and the voices of the men; observe the space that men allow themselves, physically and verbally, the male assumption that people will listen, even when the majority of the group is female. Look at the faces of the silent, and of those who speak. Listen to a woman groping for language in which to express what is on her mind, sensing that the terms of academic discourse are not her language . . . intended for her (*for it is not fitting that a woman speak in public*) . . . in breaking those silences, naming our selves, uncovering the hidden, making ourselves present, we begin to define a reality which resonates to *us*, which affirms *our* being, which allows the woman teacher and the woman student alike to take ourselves, and each other, seriously; meaning, to begin taking charge of our lives (243-245).

To ask women in every classroom they enter to talk and write regularly, to have something to say about what they read, hear, see, think, is a truly radical suggestion, for habits they form in school, we hope, will last well beyond it. This revision is not an easy thing for teachers to accomplish; it requires us to relinquish some power and control in the classroom and offer it to students, without abandoning our responsibility, to echo John Dewey, for creating situations in which real learning can take place.

What new metaphors guide us in our efforts to reconstitute the circumstances of education for women at Hollins? Certainly we are trying to get rid of the old *tabula rasa* and "empty vessel" metaphors for students, and the "ivory tower" or "rarefied atmosphere" metaphors for the academic realms where teachers live and work. In the liberating environment we are working to create, authority no longer rests solely on the shoulders of the teacher, but is shared among students and teacher alike—and let me emphasize here the relatedness of

the word "authority" and the word "authoring" in the sense
that Moffett uses it. For language is the currency of the liberating classroom, and students have as much of it to spend as do
teachers. It is open to students to share in decisions about the
direction the course takes as well as about how to proceed.
Most important, teachers do not usurp all the available linguistic space; students are invited to use language, especially written language, to explore reactions, feelings, connections between their subjects and their experience, and in the process of
drafting, revising, getting responses which move them further
into composing a reality they recognize as their own, to discover what they think. I am describing writing activities which
constitute an integral part of the ongoing process of the course,
not which run parallel to but are actually outside it. And I do
not advocate an anything-goes posture; I believe, with Adrienne Rich, that if we take women students seriously, we must
offer them a constant friendly challenge not to settle for less
than their very best. We must recognize, though, that there are
steps, stages, in getting to the point where they and we can say
with assurance that something they have done *is* their best,
and that affirming their efforts, recognizing their accomplish-
ments, and offering constructive guidance along the way is the
best way to help them get there.

I won't pretend that all faculty at Hollins are feminist, either
by conviction or in the way they see their role as teachers of
women. But certainly we have many faculty who feel a special
dedication to educating women and who recognize the political implications of the classroom scene and the student-
teacher interaction. Biochemist Sandra Boatman, a participant
from the beginning in our writing-across-the-curriculum program, sees the benefit of making student writing a central part
of her courses to be that it allows students to *be scientists* by
doing science. Thus they are actively initiated into the scientific community through adopting its discourse and, Boatman
hopes, are encouraged to see themselves and other women as
legitimate members of that community:

The women in my classes have tended to be somewhat reticent in
class; they have more or less passively received the information pro-

vided and given it back in response to direct questions. Most of them have been unwilling, unless directly asked, to volunteer, to risk anything but a safe, memorized answer. The use of several short papers based on appropriately-prepared assignments seems to be a more effective way to encourage students to engage the material actively and really use it. A good test of a student's understanding of a subject is how effectively she can explain it to another. Having her do this in writing requires her to process thoroughly and integrate the information which she has heard in lecture and discussion, read in text and literature, and observed in the laboratory. This seems to happen best when the student is asked to apply her knowledge to a different but related subject and to express her thoughts in writing, and, later, in discussion based on her writing. When the young women in my classes do this kind of thing several times, even the most reticent of them seem to become more confident and willing to risk expressing themselves.

I tie together reading, and often speaking, with the writing. The best experiences seem to occur when students read each other's work and discuss both the topic and each other's writing. If a student is aware from the start that she is not writing only for me, this makes quite a difference in the tone of her writing. Receiving a positive comment from her fellow students seems to make more of an impression than when I am the only one who has read and commented on her writing. The writing assignments also provide an excellent device for introducing students to the various kinds of literature in the discipline.

All of these writing experiences combine more or less to force the student to be a scientist and to do more than simply memorize facts. In the laboratory and in class she must actively participate; she cannot simply observe the work of others. If we provide our students with opportunities to act, think, write, and speak as scientists, they should develop the confidence to compete with anyone for jobs or positions in graduate or professional schools, or for whatever goals they may set for themselves. Perhaps, if we provide our young women who are interested in science with every opportunity to affirm themselves as scientists at the undergraduate level, they will gain the skills and self-confidence needed to overcome whatever barriers they face later. (Boatman excerpts)

Kay Richards Broschart, a sociologist at Hollins, has learned that writing promotes students' responsibility to participate actively in becoming educated. She recognizes too that students learn more thoroughly what they are asked to write about frequently:

> To engage in the practice of social science is an active undertaking. As a social scientist, I advocate that educators provide opportunities for students to experience what it means to function as a social scientist—to discover, develop, transmit, and apply the knowledge of their disciplines. As a feminist, I am especially interested in encouraging young women to become actively involved in the traditionally male spheres of activity in the social sciences, that is, in the production, development, and use of knowledge. As an educator, I am committed to transforming all students from passive recipients of education to active partners engaged in "claiming an education." Because I believe in the effectiveness of active modes of learning, all my courses currently involve a significant amount of student writing.
>
> In sum, the writing assignments [in my courses] are designed to encourage students to develop a sociological perspective (learn to think like a sociologist); engage in social inquiry (do sociology or behave like a sociologist); transmit sociological ideas and information (communicate or teach sociology); and apply sociological insights and knowledge (use sociology).
>
> Activity or experience alone, however, is not enough—it is what we do with experience that brings about learning. This is where and how writing can make a significant contribution. Writing helps us externalize and examine what we have done, what we have observed, and reflect upon it. Writing then provides a means of processing experience. Ultimately, it permits students to know what they have learned. (Broschart, excerpts)

Boatman and Broschart attest to how useful they find student writing in promoting their goals of more thorough learning by more active learners. But what benefits do students see in being asked to write a great deal? Jeanne Larsen of the Hollins English department asked them:

> I asked students in a literature class and a creative writing workshop to write for a few minutes in response to these questions: "How does writing help you learn? How does it affect you personally? Is the writing of women, or the writing experience of women, different from that of men?" Respondents were all female, and were at all class levels, including some in our M.A. program. What they wrote taught me

a lot about writing as a way of learning *through the process itself*, about their perceptions of its usefulness as a salable skill in a tight economy, and about writing as a catalyst for human liberation—the liberation of a newly known and newly confident self.

Learning through writing is active, not passive, and this would seem to be of special usefulness for American women at present. A student who stressed "writing to learn and not simply as a regurgitation" wrote, "The most exciting experience I have had academically was writing a small paper on a play, which I did not enjoy while I was reading, and discovering in the analysis process that the more I thought about it, the more worthwhile the play seemed to me. At the end, I had a real appreciation for the play." This notion of taking charge of one's own intellectual development was echoed by the student who wrote, "When I have to write a detailed paper, I have to consider how I interpret it and what it means to me."

It is the very process of writing that these women found liberating. One, who began her in-class essay with the words, "In a way, I'm almost afraid to articulate," and then crossed them out, started again as follows: "Writing takes more than it gives. But I don't actively seek pain, so some 'reward' must be there. I don't know if the continuous 'plugging away' is the result of something good that I want to propagate, or if it is the process itself that is the key. The latter is hazy and humid, but likely closer to the truth." Others agreed as to the importance of writing as a process. "Writing stimulates intellectual thought for me in that it makes me see relationships, makes me perceive similarities and differences in people, things, events, that I may have never thought of had I not been writing. Through the writing process I can fit ideas together, use my imagination, and surprise myself with the final outcome at times. By writing, I can test my theories."

The striving toward androgyny in writing on the part of one fiction writer led her to write, "I'd prefer a fusion rather than a distinction between sexes." The imaginative exploration of many modes of understanding through writing may help our students discover whole selves, even in a cultural environment that does not always support such wholeness.

Many students felt that confidence in their written expression was an area in which they had experienced real growth during their college years. Hollins' reputation for emphasizing writing "was the reason I almost said 'No' to Hollins. Writing rumors had me spooked. I was surprised I could do it and wouldn't have discovered it if I had not been forced to do it!"

Finally, and especially gratifying, there is the anonymous young woman who wrote, "In the past I have been afraid to express my own feelings, but since this class, *really*, I have felt more free to put my own ideas on paper. Now I feel that as long as I have ideas in my head, and am not afraid to express them, I could certainly do all right." (Larsen, excerpts)

It goes without saying, I hope, that what these teachers and I advocate for women students is important for men students as well. *All* students who write a lot about history will learn more history, who write about chemistry will learn more chemistry, who write poems of their own will learn more about poetry. All students deserve the best that education has to offer, and I believe that the best must always include the chance to explore, appropriate, or challenge the information and perspectives of the disciplines they study. But I argue that calling upon women students to use language in powerfully self-creating ways makes it easier for them to create selves that are free of the old mythologies. Virginia Woolf in *Three Guineas* defends women's colleges as places where a new kind of education is possible, one that does not concern itself with teaching "the arts of dominating other people" (34). Perhaps it is a luxury to teach in a women's college where we are constantly invited to consider the issues I have raised here. But it is no less critical for teachers in coeducational classrooms to consider them and to act on them; happily, the men in those classrooms will profit as well.

But make no mistake: The "vigorous criticism of old metaphors" and the adoption of new ones which challenge old systems of distributing power will have far-reaching consequences. Mary Rose O'Reilly, in a remarkable article in *College English* last year, explored the possibilities of "The Peaceable Classroom," one in which students are schooled in peace rather than for war. Using a pedagogy like the one I have advocated, she discovered that her students' experience of education had been one of sustained humiliation which had left a residue of anger, hostility, and feelings of powerlessness. She writes:

When my students tried, as they often did, to apply the insights of war literature to social analysis, trying to figure out how to defuse society, they usually found themselves rearranging traditional categories of Western thought: consensus and authority, cooperation and competition, inner and outer worlds of consciousness, male and female, intuitional and rational, mechanistic and natural. These students would tell me, for example, that our educational system has traditionally emphasized an authoritative, competitive, external, male, rational, mechanistic ordering of reality. Although this system has moved society forward in astonishing ways, they would conclude that civilization is now at a point where its very survival depends upon an integration with its lost sister/twin. . . .

What lies in our care as teachers of writing and literature is the very structure of consciousness itself, the imagination of the future. Many of the procedures we take for granted in the writing classroom—prewriting, for example, and the use of writing groups—are directed not only to changing the way our students write but to changing the way they think. The writing class today is often a student's most radical experience, a working alternative to competitive patriarchal values (111-12).

O'Reilly clearly recognizes that there is a relationship between the *way* we teach—not just *what* we teach—and the consciousness our students develop. For women students, it is not enough for us to revise our curricula to include women's history, literature, contributions to the sciences and social sciences, perspectives and experience, important as those revisions are. I believe, with O'Reilly, that writing offers dramatic possibilities for the creation of a new consciousness. I mean that every class should be a writing class, that the invitation to write, and write again, can and should be offered in all areas of the curriculum: the humanities, social sciences, science, the arts. We are familiar with the need to recover our past in these areas, to include women's perspectives and women's work in all disciplines. But the discussion is just beginning about the importance of how we conduct ourselves as teachers, how we invite women to conduct themselves as students. If we do indeed make our worlds with language, as linguists and philosophers tell us we do, then we must continue to think hard about how we invite students, especially women students, to make their world with words, and about what kind of world they and we together make. I believe that the language-centered curriculum, rich with opportunities in every discipline for women to read, write, and speak as well as listen, offers the greatest opportunity for women to become all they can be, all that those of us who care about women's education hope they will be.

Works Cited

Boatman, Sandra. "Women Writing in Science." Paper delivered as part of a panel on the Hollins writing program at the Conference on College Composition and Communication. New York, March 1984. Used with permission.

Booth, Wayne. "Rhetoric for Women." *University of Chicago Magazine*, 73, No. 3 (Winter 1981): 32, 34.

Broschart, Kay Richards. "Women Writing in the Social Sciences." Paper delivered as part of a panel on the Hollins writing program at the Conference on College Composition and Communication. New York, March 1984. Used with permission.

Dewey, John. *Experience and Education*. New York: The MacMillan Company. 1949.

Larsen, Jeanne. "Women and Writing in the Humanities." Paper delivered as part of a panel on the Hollins writing program at the Conference on College Composition and Communication. New York, March 1984. Used with permission.

Moffett, James. "Integrity in the Teaching of Writing." *Phi Delta Kappa* 64, No. 4 (December 1979): 276-279.

O'Reilly, Mary Rose. "The Peaceable Classroom." *College English* 46, No. 2 (February 1984): 103-112.

Rich, Adrienne. *On Lies, Secrets, and Silence: Selected Prose 1966-1978*. New York: W. W. Norton and Co., 1979.

Woolf, Virginia. *Three Guineas*. 1938: rpt. New York: Harcourt Brace and World, 1963.

Selected Bibliography and Suggested Further Readings

The bibliography is selective in that we have included only texts that we thought were important to either feminist or writing theory or both. Those references are drawn from both the works cited by the contributors and their suggestions for further reading. We have excluded fiction and poetry, but included references to such non-fiction as journals, diaries, and autobiographical narrative. Finally, we have included after each citation the name of the contributor in whose work the reference appeared. With this addition, we hope to provide readers with, first of all, easy access to the article in which the citation appeared; and, second, to call attention to the key texts that shaped our contributors' thinking and writing.

Selected Bibliography and Suggested Further Readings

Abel, Elizabeth, Marianne Hirsch, and Elizabeth Langland, Eds. *The Voyage In: Fictions of Female Development.* Hanover, NH: University Press of New England, 1983. (Stanger)

Abram, Morris. "Ethnics and the New Medicine." *New York Times Magazine.* 5 June 1983. 68-69, 94-100. (Horning)

Allen, Robert L. "Written English Is a 'Second Language'." *Teaching High School Composition.* Eds. Gary Tate and Edward P. J. Corbett. New York: Oxford University Press, 1970. 348-357. (Horning)

Annas, Pamela J. "Writing As Women." *Women's Studies Quarterly* 12, No. 1 (Spring 1984): 38-39. (Däumer/Runzo, Goulston)

———. "Style as Politics/Politics as Style: The Feminist Essay." Paper given at the National Women's Studies Association Conference, June 1983. (Annas)

Aston, Alexander W. *Four Critical Years: The Effects of College on Beliefs, Attitudes and Knowledge.* San Francisco: Jossey-Bass, 1977. (Horning)

———. *Preventing Students from Dropping Out.* San Francisco: Jossey-Bass, 1975. (Horning)

Baker, Sheridan. *The Complete Stylist and Handbook,* 2nd ed. New York: Harper and Row, 1980. (Caywood/Overing, Mielke)

Bechtel, Judith A. *Improving Writing and Learning.* Boston: Allyn and Bacon, 1985. (Bechtel)

Berlin, James A. "Contemporary Composition: The Major Pedagogical Theories." *College English* 44 (December, 1982): 765-777. (Mielke)

Berthoff, Ann E. *Forming Thinking Writing: The Composing Imagination.* Montclair, NJ: Boynton/Cook Publishers, Inc., 1982. (Däumer/Runzo)

———. "From Problem-Solving to a Theory of Imagination." *College English* 33 (March 1972): 636-649. (Goulston)

216   Bibliography

——. *The Making of Meaning: Metaphors, Models and Maxims for Writing Teachers.* Montclair, NJ: Boynton/Cook Publishers, Inc. 1981. (Caywood/Overing, Däumer/Runzo, Quinn)

Bleich, David. *Subjective Criticism.* Baltimore: The Johns Hopkins Press, 1978. (Däumer/Runzo)

Boatman, Sandra. "Women Writing in Silence." Paper given at the Conference on College Composition and Communication, New York, March 1984. (Faery)

Bolker, Joan. "Teaching Griselda to Write." *College English* 40 (April, 1979): 906-908. (Lavine)

Booth, Wayne. "Rhetoric for Women." *University of Chicago Magazine* 73, No. 3 (Winter 1981): 32, 34. (Faery)

Brannon, Lil, Melinda Knight, and Vera Neverow-Turk. *Writers Writing.* Montclair, NJ: Boynton/Cook Publishers, Inc. 1983. (Caywood/Overing, Quinn)

Brannon, Lil, and C. H. Knoblauch. "On Students' Rights to Their Own Texts: A Model of Teacher Response." *College Composition and Communication* 33 (May 1982): 157-166. (Frey)

Brannon, Robert, and Deborah S. David, Eds. *The Forty-Nine Percent Majority: The Male Sex Role.* Reading, MA: Addison-Wesley, 1976. (Riemer)

Britton, James, et. al. *The Development of Writing Abilities* 11-18. MacMillan Research Series. London: MacMillan Education, 1975. (Frey, Goulston)

Broschart, Kay Richards. "Women Writing in the Social Sciences." Paper given at the Conference on College Composition and Communication. New York, March 1984. (Faery)

Bruffee, Kenneth. "The Brooklyn Plan: Attaining Intellectual Growth through Peer-Group Tutoring." *Liberal Education* 64, No. 4 (December 1978): 447-468. (Goulston, Stanger)

Bunch, Charlotte. "Not By Degrees: Feminist Theory and Education." *Learning Our Way: Essays in Feminist Education.* Eds. Charlotte Bunch and Sandra Pollack. Trumansburg, NY: The Crossing Press, 1983. 248-260. (Cowell)

Chodorow, Nancy. "Being and Doing: A Cross-Cultural Examination of the Socialization of Males and Females." Gornick and Moran, 173-197. (Goulston)

——. *The Reproduction of Mothering.* Berkeley, CA: University of California Press, 1978. (Stanger)

Coles, William E., Jr. *The Plural I: The Teaching of Writing.* New York: Holt, Rinehart and Winston, 1978. (Quinn)

Cook, Stuart W. "Interpersonal and Attitudinal Outcomes in Cooperating Interracial Groups." *Journal of Research and Development in Education* 12, No. 1 (Fall, 1978): 97-113. (Frey)

Daly, Mary. *gyn/Ecology: The Metaethics of Radical Feminism.* Boston: The Beacon Press, 1978. (Annas)

Deaux, Kay. *Behavior of Women and Men.* Monterey, CA: Brooks/Cole 1976. (Goulston)

Dinnerstein, Dorothy. *The Mermaid and the Minotaur: Sexual Arrangements and Human Malaise.* New York: Harper and Row, 1976. (Goulston)

Drucker, Johanna. "Women and Language." *Poetics Journal* 4 (May 1984): 56-67. (Lavine)

Douglas, Wallace. "Rhetoric for the Meritocracy." Ohmann, 97-131. (Mielke)

Dowst, Kenneth. "The Epistemic Approach: Writing Knowing and Learning." *Eight Approaches to Teaching Composition.* Eds. Timothy R. Donovan and Ben W. McClelland. Urbana, IL: National Council of Teachers of English, 1980. 65-85. (Mielke)

Dulay, Heidi, and Marina Burt. "Remarks on Creativity in Language Acquisition." *Viewpoints on English as a Second Language.* Eds. Marina Burt, Heidi Dulay, and Mary Finocchiaro. New York: Regents Publishing Company, Inc., 1977. 95-126. (Horning)

Dulay, Heidi, and Marina Burt, and Stephen D. Krashen. *Language Two.* New York: Oxford University Press, 1982. (Horning)

Eibl-Eibesfeldt, Irenaus. *The Biology of Peace and War.* New York: The Viking Press, 1979. (Frey)

Eichenbaum, Luise, and Susie Orbach. *Understanding Women: A Feminist Psychoanalytic Approach.* New York: Basic Books, Inc., 1983. (Goulston)

Elbow, Peter. *Writing With Power: Techniques for Mastering the Writing Process.* New York: Oxford University Press, 1981. (Goulston, Quinn)

——. *Writing Without Teachers.* New York: Oxford University Press, 1983. (Quinn)

Eliot, T. S. "Tradition and the Individual Talent." *The Sacred Wood: Essays on Poetry and Criticism.* London: Methuen and Company, Ltd., 1960. 47-59. (DeShazer)

Emig, Janet. *The Composing Processes of Twelfth Graders.* Urbana, IL: National Council of Teachers of English, 1971. (Bechtel, Frey)

——. *The Web of Meaning: Essays on Writing, Teaching, Learning and Thinking.* Eds. Dixie Gosswi and Maureen Butler. Montclair, NJ: Boynton/Cook Publishers, Inc., 1983. (Däumer/Runzo)

——. "Writing as a Mode of Learning." *College Composition and*

Communication 28 (May 1977): 122-128. (Bechtel, Goulston, Quinn)

Erikson, E. A. "Womanhood and Inner Space." *Women and Analysis.* Ed. J. Strouse. New York: Dell, 1976. (Goulston)

Fisher, Bernice. "What Is Feminist Pedagogy?" *Radical Teacher*, No. 18 (1982): 20-24. (Cowell)

Fishman, Pamela M. "Interaction: The Work Women Do." *Language, Gender and Society*, Thorne et al., 89-101. (Lavine)

Flower, Linda S. *Problem Solving Strategies for Writing.* New York: Harcourt Brace Jovanovich, 1981. (Goulston, Horning)

Flower, Linda S., and John R. Hayes. "A Cognitive Process Theory of Writing." *College Composition and Communication* 35 (December 1981): 365-387. (Frey)

Frank, Francine, and Frank Anshen. *Language and the Sexes.* Albany, NY: State University of New York Press, 1983. (Lavine)

Friedman, Betty. *The Feminist Mystique.* New York: W. W. Norton and Company, Inc., 1963. (Annas)

Friedman, Susan. "Authority in a Feminist Classroom: A Contradiction in Terms?" *Feminist Pedagogy.* Madison, WI: University of Wisconsin Women's Studies Research Center, 1981. (Cowell)

Fulwiler, Toby. "The Personal Connection: Journal Writing Across the Curriculum." *Language Connections*, Fulwiler and Young, 15-31. (Perry, Quinn)

Fulwiler, Toby, and Burt Young. *Language Connections: Reading and Writing Across the Curriculum.* Urbana, IL: National Council of Teachers of English, 1982. (Perry, Quinn)

Gardner, Robert C., and Wallace E. Lambert. "Motivational Variables in Second-Language Acquisition." *Canadian Journal of Psychology* 13, No. 4 (December 1959): 266-272. (Horning)

Gilbert, Sandra M., and Susan Gubar. *The Madwoman in the Attic: The Woman Writer and the Nineteenth-Century Literary Imagination.* New Haven, CT: Yale University Press, 1979. (Frey, Stanger)

Gilligan, Carol. *In A Different Voice: Psychological Theory and Women's Development.* Cambridge, MA: Harvard University Press, 1982. (Annas, Däumer/Runzo, Goulston, Mielke, Stanger)

Goldberg, Herb. *The Hazards of Being Male: Surviving the Myth of Masculine Privilege.* New York: New American Library, 1976. (Riemer)

Gornick, Vivian, and Barbara K. Moran, Eds. *Women in Sexist Society: Studies in Power and Powerlessness.* New York: New American Library, 1971. (Goulston, Riemer)

Griffin, Susan. "Thoughts on Writing: A Diary." *The Writer on Her Work*. Ed. Janet Sternburg. New York: W. W. Norton and Company, Inc., 1980. 107-120. (Annas)

Hairston, Maxine. *A Contemporary Rhetoric*. Boston: Houghton Mifflin Co., 1974. (DeShazer)

———. "The Winds of Change: Thomas Kuhn and the Revolution in Teaching Writing." *Current Issues in Higher Education: Writing Across the Curriculum*. American Association for Higher Education No. 3 (1983-84): 4-10. (Frey, Goulston)

Hall, Roberta N. "The Classroom Climate: A Chilly One for Women?" Washington, D. C.: Project on the Status and Education of Women, 1982. (Cowell)

Hartman, Joan E., and Ellen Messer-Davidow, Eds. *Women in Print I: Opportunities for Women's Studies Research in Language and Literature*. New York: Modern Language Association, 1982. (Däumer/Runzo)

Hartsock, Nancy. "Political Change: Two Perspectives on Power." *Building Feminist Theory: Essays from "Quest."* New York: Longman, 1981. 3-19. (Cowell)

Healy, Mary K. "Using Student Writing Response Groups." *Theory and Practice in the Teaching of Composition: Processing, Distancing and Modeling*. Eds. Milo Myers and James Gray. Urbana, IL.: National Council of Teachers of English, 1983. 159-162. (Quinn)

Horning, Alice S. "A Medical Model for Teaching Basic Writing." *English Quarterly* 14, No. 2 (Summer 1981): 51-58. (Horning)

———. *Teaching Writing as a Second Language: An Inquiry*. Typescript, 1981. (Horning)

Howe, Florence. "Identity and Expression: A Writing Course for Women." *College English* 32 (May 1971): 863-871. (Goulston)

———. "A Report on Women and the Profession." *College English* 32 (May, 1971): 817-854. (Goulston)

Hull, Gloria T., Patricia Bell Scott, and Barbara Smith, Eds. *But Some of Us Are Brave: Black Women's Studies*. Old Westbury, NY: The Feminist Press, 1982. (Däumer/Runzo)

Illich, Ivan. *Deschooling Society*. New York: Harper and Row, 1971. (Mielke)

Janeway, Elizabeth. *Man's World, Woman's Place: A Study in Social Mythology*. New York: William Morrow, 1971. (Goulston)

Joll, James. *Antonio Gramsci*. New York: Viking Press, 1978. (Mielke)

Kirby, Dan, and Tom Liner. *Inside Out. Development Strategies for*

Teaching Writing. Montclair, NJ: Boynton/Cook Publishers, Inc. 1981. (Quinn)

Knoblauch, C. H., and Lil Brannon. "Teacher Commentary on Student Writing: The State of the Art." *Freshman English News* No. 2 (Fall 1981): 1-4. (Caywood/Overing)

———. "Writing as Learning through the Curriculum." *College English* 45 (September 1983): 465-74. (Perry)

Koch, Carl, and James M. Brazil. *Strategies for Teaching the Composition Process.* Urbana, IL: National Council of Teachers of English, 1978. (Quinn)

Kroll, Barry M., and John C. Schafer. "Error-Analysis and the Teaching of Composition." *College Composition and Communication* 29 (October 1978): 242-248. (Horning)

Labov, W. *The Study of Non Standard English.* Urbana, IL: National Council of Teachers of English, 1970. (Frey)

Lakoff, Robin. *Language and Woman's Place.* New York: Harper and Row, 1975. (Annas, Däumer/Runzo)

Langland, Elizabeth, and Walter Grove, Eds. *A Feminist Perspective in the Academy, The Difference It Makes.* Chicago: University of Chicago Press, 1981. (Goulston)

Larsen, Jeanne. "Women and Writing in the Humanities." Paper given at the Conference on College Composition and Communication. New York, March 1984. (Faery)

Lauter, Paul. "Working-Class Women's Literature: An Introduction to Study." Hartman and Messer-Davidow, 109-134. (Däumer/Runzo)

Lauer, Janice M., et. al., Eds. *Four Worlds of Writing.* New York: Harper and Row, 1981. (Perry)

Lifshin, Lynn, Ed. *Ariadne's Thread: A Collection of Contemporary Women's Journals.* New York: Harper and Row, 1982. (Perry)

Lindemann, Erika. *A Rhetoric for Writing Teachers.* New York: Oxford University Press, 1982. (Fuss)

Lorde, Audre. "Poetry is Not a Luxury." *Sister Outsider.* Trumansburg, NY: The Crossing Press, 1984. 36-39. (Däumer/Runzo)

———. "The Transformation of Silence into Language and Action." *Sinister Wisdom* 6 (1978): 11-15; rpt. *Sister Outsider,* 40-44. (Däumer/Runzo)

———. *Uses of the Erotic: A Rhetoric of Power.* Trumansburg, NY: The Crossing Press, 1978. (Annas)

McClelland, Ben W. *Writing Practice: A Rhetoric of the Writing Process.* New York: Longman, 1984. (Caywood/Overing, Mielke)

McDonald, Karen. "My Writing Process." *Women's Studies Quarterly* 12, No. 1 (Spring 1984): 40. (Annas)

McIntosh, Peggy, and Elizabeth Minnich. "Implications of Women's Studies for the Humanities: A Guidebook for Faculty and Curriculum Development." Unpublished manuscript. (Frey)

Macrorie, Ken. *Searching Writing: A Contextbook*. Montclair, NJ: Boynton/Cook Publishers, Inc., 1980. (Quinn)

——. *Telling Writing*. English Writing Series, 3rd ed. Montclair, NJ: Boynton/Cook Publishers, Inc., 1980. (Quinn)

Marks, Elaine, and Isabelle de Courtivron. *New French Feminisms*. Amherst, MA: University of Massachusetts Press, 1980. (Annas, Caywood/Overing, Däumer/Runzo)

Miller, Casey, and Kate Swift. "One Small Step for Genkind." *New York Times Magazine*, 16 April 1972. 36, 99-101, 106. (Freed)

Moffat, Mary Jane, and Charlotte Painter, Eds. *Revelations: Diaries of Women*. New York: Vintage Books, 1974. (Perry)

Moffat, James. *Active Voice: A Writing Program Across the Curriculum*. Montclair, NJ: Boynton/Cook Publishers, Inc., 1981. (Quinn)

——. "Integrity in the Teaching of Writing." *Phi Delta Kappan* 61, No. 4 (December 1979): 276-279. (Faery)

——. *Teaching the Universe of Discourse*. New York: Houghton Mifflin, 1968. (Frey, Quinn)

——. "Writing, Inner Speech, and Meditation." *Rhetoric and Composition*. Upper Montclair, NJ: Boynton/Cook Publishers, Inc., 1984. 65-80. (Lavine)

Moraga, Cherrie, and Gloria Anzaldúa, Eds. *This Bridge Called My Back: Writing by Radical Women of Color*, 2nd ed. New York: Women of Color Press, 1983. (Perry)

Morahan, Shirley. *A Woman's Place: Rhetoric and Readings for Composing Yourself and Your Prose*. Albany, NY: State University of New York Press, 1981. (Cowell)

Munich, Adrienne Auslander. "Feminist Criticism and the Literary Canon." Unpublished essay. 1984. (Stanger)

Murray, Donald. *Write to Learn*. New York: Holt, Rinehart and Winston, 1984. (Quinn)

——. *Learning by Teaching: Selected Articles on Writing and Teaching*. Montclair, NJ: Boynton/Cook Publishers, Inc. 1982. (Caywood/Overing)

——. "The Listening Eye: Reflections on the Writing Conference." *College English* 41 (September 1979): 13-18. (Frey)

Neilson, Brooke. "Writing as a Second Language: Psycho-linguistic

Processes in Composition." Diss., University of California at San
Diego, 1979. (Horning)

Newkirk, Thomas. "Looking for Trouble: A Way to Unmask Our
Readings." *College English* 26 (December 1984): 756-766. (Quinn)

North, Stephen M. "The Idea of a Writing Center." *College English* 46
(September, 1984): 433-446. (Mielke)

O'Leary, Virginia. *Toward Understanding Woman.* Monterey, CA:
Brooks/Cole, 1977. (Goulston)

O'Reilly, Mary Rose. "The Peaceable Classroom." *College English* 46
(February 1984): 103-112. (Faery, Frey)

Ohmann, Richard. *English in America: A Radical View of the Profession.* New York: Oxford University Press, 1976. (Däumer/Runzo,
Mielke)

Olsen, Tillie. "Silences in Literature - 1962." *Silences*, 5-21. (Lavine)

——. *Silences.* New York: Delacorte Press/Seymour Lawrence,
1978. (Annas, Däumer/Runzo)

Pascarella, Ernest, and Patrick Terenzini. "Patterns of Student-Faculty Informal Interaction Beyond the Classroom and Voluntary
Freshman Attrition." *Journal of Higher Education* 48 (1977):
540-552. (Horning)

Perl, Sondra. "The Composing Process of Unskilled College Writers."
Research in the Teaching of English 13 (December 1979): 317-
336. (Frey)

Perry, William G. *Forms of Intellectual and Ethical Development in
the College Years.* New York: Holt, Rinehart and Winston, Inc.,
1970.

Peterson, Bruce. "In Search of Meaning: Readers and Expressive Language." *Language Connections,* Fulwiler and Young, 107-122.
(Quinn)

Pleck, Joseph H., and Jack Sawyer, Eds. *Men and Masculinity.* Engle-
wood Cliffs, NJ: Prentice Hall, 1974. (Riemer)

"The Politics of Literacy," (special issue). *Radical Teacher.* No. 8
(1978). (Cowell)

Rich, Adrienne. *Of Woman Born.* New York: W. W. Norton and Company, 1976. (Däumer/Runzo)

——. *On Lies, Secrets, and Silence: Selected Prose 1966-1978.*
New York: W. W. Norton and Company, 1979. (Annas, Cowell,
Däumer/Runzo, DeShazer, Faery, Goulston, Lavine)

——. "Taking Women Students Seriously." *On Lies,* 237-245.
(Lavine)

——. "'When We Dead Awaken': Writing as Re-Vision." *On Lies,*
33-49. (Goulston, DeShazer)

———. "The Transformation of Silence into Language and Action." *Sinister Wisdom* 6 (1978): 17-24. (Däumer/Runzo)

Rico, Gabriele Lusser. *Balancing the Hemispheres: Brain Research and the Teaching of Writing.* Bay Area Writing Project Monograph. Berkeley, CA: University of California, 1980. (Quinn)

———. *Writing the Natural Way: Using Right-Brain Techniques to Release Your Expressive Powers.* Los Angeles: J. P. Tarcher, Inc., 1983. (Quinn)

Rizzo, Betty. *The Writer's Studio: Exercises for Grammar, Proofreading and Composition,* 2nd ed. New York: Harper and Row Publishers, Inc., 1982. (Horning)

Robinson, Lillian. "Treason Our Text: Feminist Challenges to the Literary Canon." *Feminist Criticism,* Showalter, 105-121. (Caywood/Overing)

Ruddick, Sara. "Maternal Thinking." *Feminist Studies* 6, No. 2 (1980): 342-367. (Däumer/Runzo)

Rosenblatt, Louise M. *The Reader, the Text, the Poem: The Transactional Theory of the Literary Work.* Carbondale, IL: Southern Illinois University Press, 1978. (Quinn)

Russ, Johanna. *How to Suppress Women's Writing.* Austin, TX: University of Texas Press, 1983. (Lavine)

Russell, Michelle. "Slave Codes and Liner Notes." Hull, et. al., 129-140. (Däumer/Runzo)

Schniedewind, Nancy. "Feminist Values: Guidelines for Teaching Methodology in Women's Studies." *Radical Teacher* No. 18 (1982): 25-28. (Cowell)

Schulz, Muriel R. "The Semantic Derogation of Woman," *Language and Sex,* Thorne and Henley, 64-75. (Cowell)

Shainess, Natalie. *Sweet Suffering: Woman as Victim.* New York: The Bobbs-Merrill Co., Inc., 1984. (Frey)

Shaughnessy, Mina P. *Errors and Expectations: A Guide for the Teachers of Basic Writing.* New York: Oxford University Press, 1977. (Frey, Goulston, Horning, Lavine)

Showalter, Elaine. "Feminist Criticism in the Wilderness." *Critical Inquiry* 8 (1984): 179-206. Rpt. in *Feminist Criticism,* Showalter, 243-270. (Caywood/Overing, Stanger)

———. *A Literature of Their Own: British Women Novelists from Brontë to Lessing.* Princeton, NJ: Princeton University Press, 1977. (Stanger)

———. Ed. *The New Feminist Criticism: Essays on Women, Literature, and Theory.* New York: Pantheon Books, 1985. (Caywood/Overing)

———. "Women and the Literary Curriculum." *College English* 32 (May 1971): 855-862. (Goulston)

Somers, Nancy. "Revision Strategies of Student Writers and Experienced Adult Writers." *College Composition and Communication* 31 (October 1980): 378-388. (Frey, Goulston)

Spender, Dale. *Man Made Language*. London: Routledge and Kegan Paul, 1980. (Annas, Däumer/Runzo)

Stanley, Julia Penelope. "Prescribed Passivity: The Language of Sexism." *Views on Language*. Eds. Reza Ordoubadian and Walburga Von Raffler Engel. Murfreesboro, TN: Middle Tennessee State University, 1975. 96-108. (Däumer/Runzo)

Stanley, Julia, and Susan J. Wolfe. "Consciousness as Style, Style as Aesthetic." *Language, Gender, and Society*, Thorne, et. al., 125-139. (Däumer/Runzo)

Stetson, Elaine. "Black Women in and out of Print." Hartman and Messer-Davidow, 87-107. (Däumer/Runzo)

———. "Studying Slavery: Some Literary and Pedagogical Considerations on the Black Female Slave." Hull, et. al., 61-84. (Däumer/Runzo)

Szilak, Dennis. "Teachers of Composition: A Re-Niggering." *College English* 39 (September 1977): 25-32. (Däumer/Runzo)

Tate, Gary, and Edward P. J. Corbett, Eds. *The Writing Teacher's Sourcebook*. New York: Oxford University Press, 1981. (Caywood/Overing)

Taylor, Sheila Ortiz. "Women in a Double Bind: Hazards of the Argumentative Edge." *College Composition and Communication* 29 (December, 1978): 385-389. (Lavine)

Thorne, Barrie, and Nancy Henley, Eds. *Language and Sex: Difference and Dominance*. Rowley, MA: Newbury House Publishers, Inc. 1975. (Cowell, Lavine)

Thorne, Barrie, Cheris Kramarae, and Nancy Henley, Eds. *Language Gender and Society*. Rowley, MA: Newbury House Publishers, Inc., 1983. (Annas, Cowell, Däumer/Runzo, Lavine)

Vetterling-Braggin, Mary, Ed. *Sexist Language: A Modern Philosophical Analysis*. Totowa, NJ: Littlefield, Adams, 1981. (Freed)

Weathers, Winston. "The Rhetoric of the Series." *Contemporary Essays on Style: Rhetoric, Linguistics, Criticism*. Ed. Glen A. Love and Michael Payne. Glenview, IL: Scott, Foresman and Co., 1969. 21-27. (DeShazer)

Weathersby, Rita Preszler. "Education for Adult Development: The Components of Qualitative Change." *New Directions for Higher Education*: Vol. 29 *Educating Learners of All Ages*. Eds. Elinor

Greenburg, et. al. San Francisco: Jossey-Bass, Inc., Publishers, 1980. 9-22. (Goulston)

West, Candace, and Don H. Zimmerman. "Sex Roles, Interruptions and Silences in Conversation." *Language and Sex*, Thorne and Henley, 105-129. (Lavine)

———. "Small Insults: A Study of Interruptions in Cross-Sex Conversations between Unacquainted Persons." *Language, Gender and Society*, Thorne, et al, 102-117. (Lavine)

Winterowd, W. Ross. *The Contemporary Writer. A Practical Rhetoric.* New York: Harcourt Brace Jovanovich, 1981. (Quinn)

Wolff, Cynthia Griffin. "A Mirror for Men: Stereotypes of Women in Literature." *Massachusetts Review* 13 (1972): 205-218. (Riemer)

Woolf, Virginia. *A Room of One's Own.* 1929. Rpt. New York: Harcourt, Brace and World, Inc., 1957. (Annas, Lavine)

———. *Three Guineas.* 1938. Rpt. New York: Harcourt, Brace and World, 1963. (Faery)

Zeiger, William. "The Exploratory Essay: Enfranchising the Spirit of Inquiry in College Composition." *College English* 47 (September 1985): 454-466. (Quinn)

Ziv, Nina D. "The Effect of Teacher Comments on the Writing of Four College Freshmen." *New Directions in Composition Research.* Eds. Richard Beach and Lillian S. Bridwell. New York: The Guildford Press, 1984. (Frey)

Notes on Contributors

PAMELA J. ANNAS is an Associate Professor of English at the University of Massachusetts/Boston. She has published articles on contemporary women poets, the teaching of writing, and science fiction. Her book, *A Disturbance in Mirrors: The Poetry of Sylvia Plath*, will be published by Greenwood Press. She is a member of the editorial collective of *The Radical Teacher*. This article, along with one in *College English*, (April 1985), was written on a Mina Shaughnessy Scholars Grant.

JUDITH BECHTEL is an Associate Professor of Literature and Language and Director of the Composition Program at Northern Kentucky University. There she teaches writing and literature. She has published *Improving Writing and Learning: A Handbook for Teachers in All Classes* and, along with Bettie Franzblau, *Reading in the Content Areas: Science*. Recently she has completed a new book, *The Best of Both Worlds: A Composition Textbook for Students with Word Processors*. She has also given numerous presentations and workshops in composition theory.

CYNTHIA L. CAYWOOD is an Assistant Professor of English at the University of San Diego. In addition to directing the Writing Center, she teaches Composition, History of the English Language, Eighteenth Century British Literature and Women's Literature. She has published essays on Henry Mackenzie, Jane Austen and writing; she has also led workshops on writing across the curriculum. Currently she is pursuing research in writing theory and Eighteenth-century women writers.

PATTIE COWELL is an Associate Professor of English at Colorado State University. She has been teaching writing and literature since 1972 and women's studies courses since 1978. She has published several articles on women writers and an anthology of *Women Poets in Pre-Revolutionary America.* More recently, she co-edited *Critical Essays on Anne Bradstreet* with Ann Stanford.

ELIZABETH DAUMER is a graduate student in the Department of English of Indiana University and presently writing her dissertation on "Masculinity and Modern Literary Theory." From 1983 to 1985 she has worked as assistant editor of *College English;* her frequent experiences teaching writing classes have convinced her of the need for feminist writing pedagogy.

MARY DeSHAZER is an assistant professor of English at Xavier University. She has published articles on May Sarton, Louise Bogan, H. D., and other women poets. She has also written about feminist educational reforms and sexism and language. At present DeShazer's book on women poets and creative inspiration *Inspiring Women & Re-Imagining the Must* is forthcoming from Pergamon Press.

REBECCA BLEVINS FAERY is Coordinator of Writing at Hollins College, a private liberal arts college for women in Virginia, where she teachers writing, directs the Writing Center, and coordinates the college's program in writing across the curriculum. She was a Fellow of the NEH-Iowa Institute on Writing in 1980 and has published poems, essays, and reviews in various books and periodicals.

ALICE F. FREED is Associate Professor of Linguistics at Montclair State College in New Jersey. She is also a member of the Women's Studies Advisory Board. She teaches courses in both Linguistics and Women's Studies. Her publications are in English syntax and semantics as well as in male and female speech and sexism in language. Her current research is on the persistence of gender-stereotyping in language.

OLIVIA FREY is Assistant Professor of English and Director of the Writing Program at St. Olaf College in Northfield, Minnesota. She is currently doing research on the links between feminism and peace and on writing process theory and pedagogy. Her most recent publication is "The Pedagogy of Peace," *Peace and Change Journal*, (Spring 1985).

DIANA J. FUSS is a doctoral candidate in the English Language and Literature program at Brown University. She is writing her dissertation on maternal discourse in the works of Jane Austen, Mary Shelley, and Emily Brontë and teaches in the Brown writing program and Writing Center. She is also at work on an article deconstructing the essentialist/non-essentialist debate in feminist theory.

WENDY GOULSTON is an assistant professor at Empire State College where she teaches writing, literature, and interdisciplinary courses. She has published articles on Sir Philip Sidney, Shakespeare's *As You Like It* and *Twelfth Night*, and on group dynamics in the classroom. Her research is currently focused on women's experiences as writers, particularly the relationship between gender and writing anxiety.

ALICE HORNING is an assistant professor of rhetoric at Oakland University. Currently she is researching the relationship between reading and writing from a psycholinguistic perspective. She is also completing work on a manuscript entitled *Teaching Writing as a Second Language*, a discussion of the relationship between learning to write and second language learning. She has published in *College English, Teaching English in the Two-Year College*, and *Journal of Advanced Composition*.

ANN LAVINE, a former high school writing teacher, is presently studying at Illinois State University and teaching composition.

ROBERT MIELKE teaches writing and literature at Northeast Missouri State. In addition to his interest in Women's Studies and Writing Theory, his intellectual activities embrace W. D. Howells and pop culture representations of nuclear weaponry.

GILLIAN R. OVERING is an associate professor of English at Wake Forest University where she teaches Old English, History of the Language, Linguistics, Women's Studies and Composition. She has conducted writing workshops and has published essays on Old English poetry and composition. Her current research interests include linguistics and Anglo-Saxon poetics, and writing theory.

MICKEY PEARLMAN is Assistant Professor of English at Iona College, where she teaches Basic and Advanced Writing, Modern American Literature and Major British Writers. She has contributed several biographical/critical entries to the forthcoming *British Women Authors* (Ungar) and is finishing a book entitled *Reinventing Reality: Patterns and Characters in the Novels of Muriel Spark.*

DONNA M. PERRY is Assistant Professor of English at William Paterson College where she teaches writing, literature, and Women's Studies. She has written and directed a play based on the letters of nineteenth century working women, conducted workshops on writing across the curriculum, and presented papers at numerous conferences. She chaired a session on "Issues of Race, Class, and Gender in the Feminist Classroom" at the 1985 National Women's Studies Association Conference and has just completed a chapter on "Evaluating Students' Writing" for a forthcoming faculty handbook on writing across the curriculum.

MARY A. QUINN teaches Composition, British and Continental Romanticism, American, and Contemporary World Literature at the University of San Diego. From 1980-1984 she served as a teacher-consultant with the South Coast Writing Project (an affiliate of the National Writing Project) while completing her graduate studies at UC Santa Barbara. During 1983-1984 she was Associate Director of SCWriP. Her scholarship focuses on the British Romantics, and her articles on Shelley and his circle have appeared in *English Language Notes, Studies in English Literature, The Explicator;* further work is forthcoming in *The Wordsworth Circle* and the *Keats-Shelley Journal.*

SUSAN RADNER is an Associate Professor of English and Women's Studies and Coordinator of the Women's Studies Program at William Paterson College. She has published articles on women and literature and women and language in *Frontiers, Radical Teacher,* and *Iowa English Bulletin,* and presented papers on these subjects at the annual conferences of the National Women's Studies Association.

JAMES DOUGLAS RIEMER is an Assistant Professor at Marshall University, where he teaches Composition as well as Twentieth-century Fiction and Science Fiction/Fantasy. His current research interests involve the plays of Sam Shepard and applying a men's studies approach to American literature. He has published essays on James Branch Cabell and on sex roles in science fiction/fantasy.

SANDRA RUNZO, a graduate student in the Department of English at Indiana University, has taught a variety of basic skills and experimental writing classes. She is writing a dissertation on Adrienne Rich's poetry and is a member of the *Feminist Teacher* Editorial Collective.

CAROL A. STANGER is Director of the Writing Center at John Jay College of Criminal Justice. Previously, she headed national and regional institutes in collaborative learning, and co-directed the conference, "Collaborative Learning and the Reinterpretation of Knowledge," held at Yale in 1984.

Index